My First 250 Years

The Story of the Hertzog Homestead

K. Scott Hertzog

Masthof Press

219 Mill Road
Morgantown, PA 19543
www.masthof.com

DEDICATION

This book is dedicated to my father, Kenneth Buch Hertzog. Without his research and passion for family history, this book would not exist. This book is also dedicated to my wife, who has read many drafts and stood by me as I worked on it and encouraged me to continue, and my children, Taicha and Kiefer, who give me a reason to pass on this knowledge.

CONTENTS

THE HERTZOG HOMESTEAD FAMILY TREE

1744 | Elias Meyer buys the land from William Penn's Sons. | 1760

1760 | Peter Meyer inherits land from Elias; builds the log house, the existing barn, and a 30 x15 foot 1 story house. | 1786

1786 | Jacob N. Metzler buys the plantation from Peter Meyer; builds the carriage house. | 1820

1820 | Jacob H. Metzler expands the barn and converts the house into 2 stories. | 1859

1859 | Jacob S. Metzler builds the tobacco shed. | 1894

1894 | Daniel Buch marries Lizzie Metzler, moves onto farm, and expands the carriage house and barn. | 1945

1945 | Elmer M. Buch and Jacob M. Buch build the block butcher house. | 1976

1976 | Kenneth Buch Hertzog buys the farm 200 years after his great grandfather. | 2003

2003 | K. Scott Hertzog acquires the farm; converts main house into the bed and breakfast, later expanding it to include the carriage house.

ACKNOWLEDGEMENTS

All stories begin somewhere. It does not matter whether it is the life of a house, the life of the land, or the life of men, women, and children who lived there. The Jacob Metzler Plantation, or as it is known today The Hertzog Homestead Bed and Breakfast, stands on the shoulders of the men and women who have pulled her stone by stone from the earth and shaped her into who she is today.

She was birthed into existence by Peter Meyer, was Jacob N. Metzler's Plantation, was expanded under Jacob H. Metzler, was divided between the twins Jacob and John, became the Buch Farm, and finally the Hertzog Homestead.

She evolved, grew, and changed to meet the needs of the times and the families that lived in her. The Jacob N. Metzler family has lived between her walls for 9 generations. She is what she is today because of the many who have gone before.

The same is true for this book. I stand on the shoulders of those who have walked the path before me, and who in many cases did much of the ground work.

The first person I must acknowledge is my father, Kenneth Buch Hertzog, who imparted the genealogical bug in me. He did the leg work on much of the family's genealogy, and his collection of deeds, papers, and other family artifacts was instrumental in pulling together this book. I remember him helping me on an eighth grade family tree for Art Reise's history class and also helping me conduct a recording of my grandmother. This was my first foray into the history of my family and appreciating it. Years later as an adult, he helped fill in the gaps as I did some of my own genealogical work. A majority of the deeds I reference and genealogical work I use are my father's. In many ways this book would be not be what it is without him. And I miss him. This book would have made him proud.

Jane Metzler Zimmerman, who grew up on the farm next to the Jacob Metzler Plantation, was also vital in providing information and helping fill in the gaps. Her book *Jacob Metzler and His Descendants* helped provide some of the information found on these pages. She helped provide a framework for understanding some of the more recent history of the Metzlers.

Ken Miller, whose is the foremost expert on Lime Kilns in the county, helped me track down and discover the lime kiln that lay in ruins on the property and helping me understand better how they functioned. Someday I hope to excavate that area.

The extended Oberholtzer family helped me better understand my great uncles, Jacob and Elmer. Their stories helped flesh out the people who lived here and also helped find the lime kiln location. Sam Oberholtzer was especially helpful as he told stories of working on the property in the 1950s and 1960s while we walked around the farm. Mary Jane and Rueben have especially been wonderful neighbors and shared many stories as well.

Lem Metzler, who, though not of the Jacob Metzler line, helped me understand better the European history of the Metzlers. The 250th Metzler reunion also helped in understanding the rich background of the Metzler Family. He was also instrumental in helping me edit various drafts of this book.

Nico Patel, my eight cousin from Germany, was instrumental in expanding my understanding both the Metzlers and the Meyers in Germany. My e-mails and discussions with him have been enlightening and have changed the way I viewed my ancestors.

Lisa Mayo, who read through the manuscript with the eye of an English teacher. Even though I am of the same profession, it is amazing how much one misses when so close to the material.

The Cocalico Historical Society, the Lancaster Historical Society, and the Mennonite Historical Society all contributed in the research for this book.

The late Arlene E. Hertzog, my grandmother, helped me to flesh out rural Pennsylvania life in the 1920s and 1930s and understand the area surrounding the farm. Many of the family photos come from her.

Marlene Buch also provided much of the photographic evidence in this book. Many of the Buch Family photographs are from her collection.

And my mother, Arlene S. Hertzog, who raised us on the Jacob Metzler farm, was instrumental in encouraging us kids to pursue higher education. Were it not for her persistent guidance and encouragement, this book would not be here.

And lastly my wife, Kristen, who has encouraged me as I worked on this endeavor, watched our children while I did research, and was an all-around support. I love you more than I'll ever be able to adequately express.

FORWARD

My ambition in putting together this book is to better appreciate the roles of people surrounding the Jacob Metzler Plantation on which I grew up. I wanted to give a context for the buildings, the times, and the people who lived here.

Researching the Jacob Metzler Plantation has sent me scurrying to the many historical societies in Lancaster County, PA and scouring the countless documents my father owned and other family members had. It has been both immensely rewarding and frustrating at times.

I am sure some will find things in here that I perhaps misinterpreted or perhaps have some clarification on a point I have made. This edition of the book is not necessarily definitive, and I welcome the chance to make it more so. Please e-mail me at thehertzogs@gmail.com or write me at 470 West Metzler Road, Ephrata, PA 17522.

Some of you reading might also have stories that relate to the people I have mentioned in this book. I want to know these stories in order that I might better understand the people and better convey that in future editions of this book. If that is you, please contact me using the information I provided above.

All pictures are of the public domain unless noted elsewhere or are digital copies of pictures my family owns.

I hope that in someway I have helped make the history of the Jacob Metzler Plantation come alive. Thank you for reading.

Scott Hertzog

The Time Before Settlers

K. Scott Hertzog

The Native American Fantasies

The summer of 1981 bore down dry and hot. For the first time since we had moved into the plantation house, the well that serviced it could not provide enough water, forcing my father to dig another and forcing us to use the outhouse that was used regularly up until the early 1960s.

On these heat laden days, my mother made my brother Doug and I do our chores in the morning, such as weeding the garden and mowing, while it was cooler, so that we could play during the hot part of the day. Sometimes this took us to a watering hole that my father had dug out with his green skid loader. Because of it's black liner, swimming there was like taking a bath on the hottest of summer days. If we really wanted to stay cool, my brother and I would hang out in the barn.

Fueled by stories of Westerns, we would play cowboys and Indians. In the northern most mow of the barn, the place where straw and hay were stored, Doug and I would sometimes line up bales in a fort formation, complete with escape tunnels, but our best defense lay in the ventilation slits that dotted the northern most wall. Armed with tobacco lathe and stick guns, we pressed ourselves against the cool stone wall and peered out across the neighbor's barley field. In our imagination's eye, we could see the dust kicked up in the the distance and hear the whoops and yells from the Indian posse on horseback, thundering our way. Like the Alamo, we slipped our pretend rifles through the holes and prepared to make our last stand.

Despite these childhood fantasies, the Native American reality in the area of Lancaster, Pennsylvania played out quite a bit differently.

The Indian Presence in Lancaster County

To really understand the Native American presence surrounding the Hertzog Homestead, we need to first consider the

A mastodon similar to the one found in Ephrata, PA.

landscape. The area is filled with gradual rolling hills composed of limestone soil. The Conestoga Creek (or River as we called it) is the closest body of water and is a tributary to the Susquehanna River. These hills and the river lay in the bowl between the Furnace Hills to the north, the closest of which is the Ephrata Mountain, and the Welsh Mountains to the South East. Neither of these are truly mountains in the real sense of the word, acting more like big hills. The real lack of physical boundaries, since the shallowness of the Susquehanna to the west did not provide a real barrier, made Lancaster County easily accessible to the Native Americans.[1]

The earliest Indians settled in the Washington Boro area, about 20 miles from the Hertzog Homestead. Their settling in this location made sense since the growing season was 205 days, almost month longer than in the area surrounding the homestead farm. When the fertile soil, fair climate, plenty of game, and river access are considered, its clear why major Indian settlements happened in the Conestoga and Washington Boro areas. Lancaster's soils are rich limestone, well drained, and excellent for agriculture.[2]

Indian artifacts my father collected, allegedly from the farm.

Archeological digs indicate that small settlements existed along the shores of the Susquehanna river as early as sometime between 10,000 and 8,000 BC. These groups of Indians were called Paleo (old or ancient) Indians. While there are no known settlements near the Hertzog Homestead, these Indians most likely roamed the area in search of game like the arctic shrew, the northern bog lemming, caribou, and even mastodon. The remains of one such mastodon were found near Ephrata less than two miles away from the homestead.[3]

Two other periods of Indian culture existed in the Washington Boro area: The Archaic Indians, who were hunters, fishers, and gatherers (8000 BC to 1000 BC) and the Woodland Period Indians, who seemed more focussed on horticultural and village life (1000 BC to 1550 AD).[4]

The era of Indians that plays most prominently into the white man's arrival is that of the Susquehannock Indians (1575 AD to

1675 AD). The first written account of the Indians in Lancaster county begins when Captain John Smith, of the Pocahontas fame, encountered a group of 60 warriors, presumably from the area of Washington Boro.[5] By the late 1600's, the only prominent Indian settlement, and remnants of the Susquehannocks, and Senecas existed at Conestoga.[6]

The Native American Presence Near the Hertzog Homestead

This paints a short history of the Indian presence in Lancaster County. But how do these people figure into the history of this property? My family has a smattering of arrowheads, axeheads, and other Indian artifacts that my father collected while farming the land, so obviously they roamed the area.

Perhaps the only reference to Indians specifically in the area of the plantation comes from H. M. J. Klien. When German settlers first arrived in Lancaster County, they found the area full of tall trees, but they were unhindered in their travel since the forests lacked undergrowth. He concluded that the "Indians were never numerous; 'scarcely more than half a dozen families were ever to be found in one place;' yet the Indian custom of burning scrubby underwood 'made it not a difficult matter to drive a cart for long distances through woods in all directions.'"[7]

The rest of the information we have is a bit more speculative and conjecture. While it is not farfetched to believe that Indians from the Paleo-Indian, Archaic, and Woodland periods traveled and hunted the lands surrounding the Hertzog Homestead, there is little concrete proof that they settled here. If anything, it seems a fairer bet that the Susquehannocks, who later merged into the Conestoga Indians along with the Seneca and other Indian tribes, paddled up this river since the hub of their society surrounded the mouth of the Conestoga River.

Yet there are stories, oral tradition and rumors, that wend their way down through families. Many times there tend to be a kernel of truth in them.

The Nearby Indian Path

The Conestoga River lies a half mile away from the Homestead. Turtle Hill Road travels from Brownstown along the Conestoga Creek until in ends at the Farmersville bridge. Fabric shop owner Emma Martin, who lives on the corner of Turtle Hill Road and Snyder Road, tells that her grandfather remembers being told that Turtle Hill Road was once an Indian path. The road remains close to the creek, following its contours, yet takes advantages of the high ridges nearby; this suggests a truth in this piece of oral history. This would allow the Indian travelers to keep their moccasins dry. Historically many Indian pathways were eventually converted to roads.[8]

The Indian Trading Post

Joel Buch, a Social Studies teacher at Conestoga Valley High

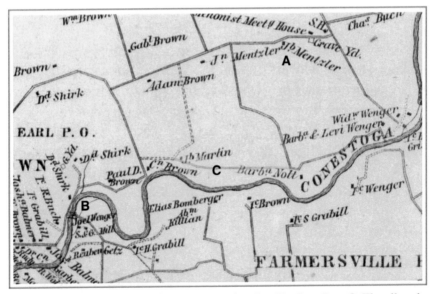

A. The Hertzog Homestead B. The alleged Indian Trading Post C. The alleged Indian path

School, teaches local history and shared that his grandfather once heard stories of an Indian trading post near the juxtaposition of West Farmersville Road, East Main Street in Brownstown, and Turtle Hill Road. This story has some merit since the Indian settlement in Conestoga was predominately a trading town and situated where the Conestoga River spills into the Susquehanna.[9] It would be easy to imagine them traveling up the river to this trading post, and other trading posts like this.

The trading post would have been run by the Dutch or the French, who were enlisted by the Governor of Pennsylvania to conduct fur trade. At this post, Conestogas would have brought furs to exchange for other goods. An inventory list from Conestoga area trading posts indicates some of the items the Indians would have offered for trade and gives insight as to what sort of wildlife was roaming the woods at the time. Pelts and skins from white tailed deer, elk, foxes, bobcats, raccoons, and bear were common and exchanged for items like gunpowder, blankets, buckshot, buttons, and ribbon.[10]

The Indian Cave

The aforementioned Emma Martin also recounts a story from her grandfather of a cave that had Indian markings on its walls. The entrance to the cave collapsed at some point. It was located along the Conestoga Creek between Farmersville bridge and the Talmage bridge. Thomas Weaver, former school teacher at Metzler's one room school house from 2004 to 2010, attempted to verify the story, and talked to elderly locals who thought they too remembered a cave, but the existence of such a cave remains unverified.

How This Impacted the Hertzog Homestead

Native Americans definitely crossed the lands of the Hertzog Homestead. They cleared the brush in the area so that when Peter Meyer, and later Jacob Metzler, continued to clear the land for farming, their job was easier because of them. While there were Indians in the area when Elias Meyer purchased the land, by the time the earliest buildings of the Hertzog Homestead were built, they lived mostly in the Conestoga area 20 miles away.

K. Scott Hertzog

It Begins With Elias

The Reformation Upheaval in Europe

People live in the context of history; history shapes their lives, the way they lived, and where they went. The same is true for those who shaped the Hertzog Homestead. Elias Meyer's journey to Pennsylvania and to land on which the Homestead exists has its roots in the Protestant Reformation.

While many people and events from the 13th through 14th centuries contributed to the Protestant Reformation, its watershed moment occurred in 1517. Dissatisfaction with the Catholic Church and their practices grew during the Middle Ages. The Catholic Priest Martin Luther had a problem in particular with the sale of indulgences. As a result, he nailed the *Ninty-Five Theses* to the door of Wittenberg's church, in Wittenberg, Germany. These Theses in particular propounded two central beliefs—that the Bible is the central religious authority and that humans may reach salvation only by their faith and not by their deeds. This ignited revolution that was as much political as it was spiritual.

Political leaders gained economically if the land was no longer subservient to the Catholic Church, since they no longer had to pay taxes and tithes. They rallied around Luther and thus helped his cause. When the Catholic Church responded to Luther's Theses by excommunicating him, he sought sanctuary with Elector Frederick the Wise, who established the University at Wittenberg where Luther studied and who just happened to be the son of the Prince of Saxony. The Prince of Saxony saw an opportunity to kick against the goads of the Roman Empire and did so.

These events led many other reformers to step out of the shadows. Notable among these is Ulrich Zwingli, a former priest as well, who inadvertently spawned the Anabaptist movement. In Zurich, Switzerland, Zwingli taught salvation by grace, believed priests should be able to marry, rejected transubstantiation, and practiced the Lord's Supper separate from the mass. He was in agreement with Luther on these things. A bit more zealous than

Luther, he also rejected the use of fine arts in services.

Zwingli lead the Grossmünster Protestant Church in Zurich. Several of his followers, particularly Felix Manz and Conrad Grebel, thought he was moving too slow in his reforms. This came to a head when Zwingli supported the continuing practice of infant baptism, but Grebel argued for an adult believer's baptism. Zwingl's position played into politics as well since church membership, citizenship, and therefore taxes were tied to infant baptism. The church council insisted Grebel and Manz stop

The Grossmünster ("great minster") a Romanesque-style Protestant church in Zurich, Switzerland.

meeting and propagating this teaching against infant baptism. On January 21, 1525, Grebel and Manz responded by meeting once again and baptizing each other. John Ruth writes that George Blaurock was present at this meeting and was the first to request baptism. The movement this started spread throughout Zurich and the surrounding countryside and its participants became known as Anabaptists, meaning "rebaptizers".

Zwingli led the now protestant Zurich in a decisive response. A city decree issued in 1525 called all Anabaptists to forsake the teaching of Grebel and Manz under the threat of imprisonment, torture, and death. Following this decree, Manz became one of the first Anabaptist leaders martyred, an act carried out by drowning in January of 1527. Despite the threats and the

Les Grandes Misères de la guerre (The Great Miseries of War) depicting the Palatinate Wars by Jacques Callot, 1632

following persecution, the Anabaptist teachings spread throughout Switzerland and into southern Germany.

By 1635, most of the Anabaptists had left the cities and resided in the countryside where they lived in relative freedom. Zurich decided to get rid of the Anabaptists throughout the entire canton. After learning that public execution led to martyrs, Zurich's leadership tried a different tactic and imprisoned these Christians. There they were tortured and neglected which often led to death. This forced the remaining Anabaptists flee the Zurich area.

The Anabaptists found refuge in Germany. Elector Karl Ludwig, who ruled much of the Palatinate, offered tolerance to persecuted groups. This was not purely a benevolent act, but rather was in part a result of the Thirty Year War (1618 through 1648) which had raged through central Europe and took it greatest toll on the Palatinate. Much of the population had been reduced and the countryside was laid to waste. The Swiss Anabaptists settled here. Being a Palatinate territory meant that it was part of the historical area belonging to the Holy Roman Empire. Quite literally, it was a territory under the jurisdiction of Count Palatine.

The Swiss settled in less than perfect conditions. Ludwig only allowed them to worship in their own homes, they could admit no one else from other denominations into their meetings,

Eppingen, Germany

and could not rebaptize people who had already been baptized. But there were nonspiritual conditions as well. Trades and land ownership were restricted, and the Swiss settlers incurred special taxes.

Despite these conditions, the refugees' lives were not threatened. Therefore, Karl Ludwig's plan to repopulate Germany was successful. In fact it eventually led to an overpopulation of the area. Ludwig died in 1685. It was at this point that French King Louis the XIV saw an opportunity to acquire more land.[1]

War Rumbled in Eppingen

War rumbled in Eppingen, Germany, and the villagers trembled in fear. The German armies fortified this southern Palatinate town, armed with matchlocks (a self-firing gun) and a smattering of the new fangled flintlocks retrofitted with socket bayonets. These could skewer a man in close combat. As supplies to the French army waned, the Germans defeated the them using these, rather than the traditional plug bayonets.

The nine year war against the Holy Roman Empire started when French King Louis the XIV's armies attacked Philippsburg, Germany, on 27 September 1688, and town after town began to fall. The Germans, backed by the Holy Roman Empire, retaliated in force, stopping the French advancement. When it became clear that that the war would not be won quickly, the French armies burned the fields as they retreated. Since armies acquired their provisions from people and land around them, this left the German armies with few resources and the German people hungry.

The town of Eppingen became part of the County Palatine of Rhine in 1436. After the death of Karl Ludwig, Philip William became Count Palatine in 1685 and established Eppingen as the central storage facility for the German Army in 1688. Johann Wilhelm became Count Palatine in 1690 and during the last three years of the war, from 1695 to 1697, he built the Eppingen Lines of Defense, which served as large defending walls against the French Raiders.[2] The French eventually withdrew and signed the Treaty of Ryswick. It was into this upheaval that Elias Meyer was born.

Elias Meyer's Journey to America

Elias Meyer, whose last name is also written as Myer, Maÿer, or Moyer, was born December 11, 1697 in Eppingen to Hans Mayer and his wife Elizabetha. On February 2, 1716 or 1717, he married Louisa Frederika Globman, daughter of Johnnes Globman, also from Eppingen.[3]

When King Louis burned the fields as his armies retreated, this not only impacted the German armies, but also had long lasting, repressive effects on the German farm owners and Swiss Anabaptists. It left the region in poverty, sickness, starvation, and cold in the decades that followed.[4] Apparently, after 10 years of trying to eek out a living, Elias Meyer had enough.

In 1681, quaker William Penn acquired the lands known as "Penn's Woods". King Charles the II owed Penn's father a favor; Pennsylvania was given to William to settle the King's debt. Penn needed people to live in this land so that Pennsylvania would become lucrative and not force him into poverty.

William Penn

Perhaps because of the influence of William Penn's German mother, Penn made several visits to the Rhine Valley in which Eppingen lies. He printed leaflets and distributed them throughout the valley, which promised takers 100 acres of land for 2 English pounds and a low annual rent.[5] In the midst of the hardship of living in Germany, this had to look appealing. Elias decided to take his wife and four young children, Vincent (age 6) John (age 4), Agnes Barbara (age 2), and Maria Eva (age 1) and head to Pennsylvania.

In 1727, Elias and Louisa packed up, and headed west to the Rhine River. Here they caught a boat to Rotterdam in the Netherlands. The trip to Rotterdam lasted several weeks, mostly because of trying to comply with the regulations of the various principalities that existed along the Rhine.[6] After several weeks in Rotterdam, they boarded the *William and Sarah* and began their journey to America.

It was a costly trip. Elias paid anywhere from five to ten pounds sterling silver for the adults and half the price for his children.[7] It is difficult to determine what this cost would be in today's money. The pound fluctuated quite a bit during this time. However, we get an idea what it was worth in labor. If a family could not pay for their passage, it typically resulted in about 7

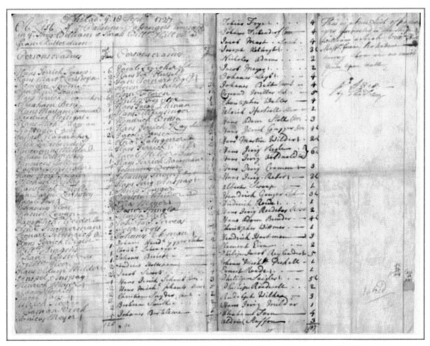

The William and Sarah Passenger List. Elias Meyer's name is highlighted.

years of indentured servitude once they reached the shores of the new world.

The ship first sailed to Dover, England, an 8 to 14 day trip, where, after another delay, it picked up additional immigrants. By the time they arrived in Philadelphia, the *William and Sarah* had 113 men on board, totaling with their families 400 people.

The *William and Sarah* left port in early Summer, taking advantage of the calmer seas and balmy weather of the Northern Atlantic Ocean. Leaving in late June, the trip took about eleven weeks. The *William and Sarah* arrived in Philadelphia on September 18, 1727. In general, traveling conditions were not optimal. Typically, ships were crowded, food was limited, and disease was imminent. Many passengers came down with ship fever (typhus), dysentery, smallpox, and scurvy.[8] A journey such as this foreshadowed the years ahead for Elias and Louisa and how hard it would be to pioneer an unsettled area.

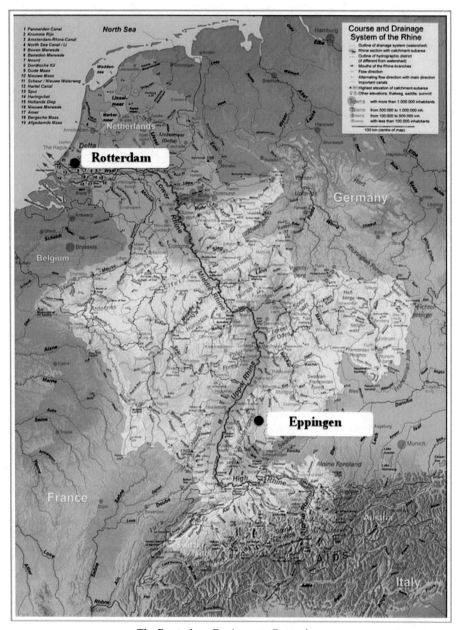

The Route from Eppingen to Rotterdam

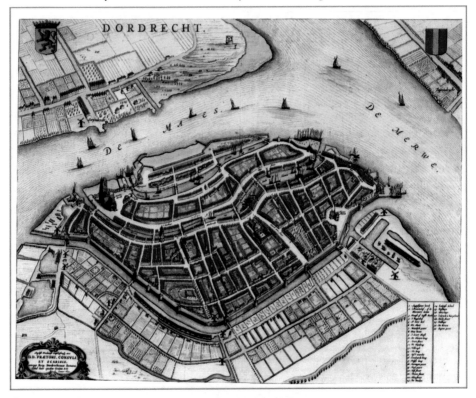

Rotterdam in the 1600s

A boat similar to the William and Sarah

The New World Experience

One can imagine Elias arriving in Philadelphia after the eleven week journey, and his relief knowing that he and his family had survived.   Standing on the deck with his wife and two children as the *William and Sarah* sailed up the Delaware Bay and then as it was pushed into dock, he had to hope that the heartaches of the old world were past.

Though anxious to disembark, he and the other 400 passengers had to wait for the doctor, who lived down the street a half of block. Upon boarding the boat, the doctor checked to make sure all were healthy and had no contagious diseases. Apparently only 51 of the 114 men on board were deemed "qualified". The rest lay sick on board. Only four had died during the voyage.[9]

Those who were unqualified or contagious were taken by rowboat down the bay to Province Island until they became well or died.[10] Elias and his family were apparently cleared, a process that took three days.

On September 21, 1727, Elias, along with all the men, followed the captain down the cobblestone street two blocks to the Customs House. On entering, he saw the Pennsylvania officials seated behind a long desk. The ship's master, William Hill, signed his name first. Elias stood in line with the rest of the men, and when it was his turn, he signed his name along with the number of dependents that were with him. After this occurred, he went back to the boat where Louisa, Vincent, and John were finally allowed to disembark.[11]

This Land is My Land

The next stop typically would have been to walk down the street a few blocks to the land office, where those who wanted to purchase land in Lancaster County were shown maps of forests that had been surveyed and the parts of County which had not. If Elias had wanted to buy land, he would first have had to sign a warrant which would have given him the right to have a surveyor take a survey of the land. He would have travelled, possibly with his family, with the surveyor to Lancaster County. Once the land was surveyed, he would have had to walk back to Philadelphia, pay for the land, and then receive a deed.[12]

There is one problem with this supposition. Elias did not get a warrant for land until June 7, 1738, almost 11 years after he arrived in America. Why? What was he doing during the ten years before he finally received a warrant for his land?

One possibility is that he and his family perhaps did not have the funds for the passage to America. If this was the case, they would have agreed to work as indentured servants for 3 to 7 years. People who did this were known a "Redemptioners."[13] Upwards towards 50 to 70 percent of American colonists were indentured, making this possibility likely.

Elias and Louisa lived in Earl Township during these years. During this period, they also added Elias Meyer Junior to their family, who was born about 1731, and Peter, who was born June 13, 1735. Both was baptized at Muddy Creek Lutheran Church in Earl Township. This is now a part of East Cocalico Township. In addition to these two sons and the two who traveled with them from the old world, Elias and Louisa had two daughters as well: Margaret Meyer, born in 1733, and Catherine, born in 1738. He seems established in the area with a family of eight.

The year Catherine was born, Elias travelled down to Philadelphia and signed a warrant for a 136 acre tract of land on June 7th, 1738. The property was surveyed on May 29, 1744. The land was officially granted to him on November 16, 1744 by John, Thomas, and Richard Penn, the sons of the late William Penn. Once the warrant was granted, he probably began the work of clearing land.[14] The fact that the Conestoga Creek runs through his land was no accident and may hint as to what Elias was doing during those eleven years in which he owned no property. He is

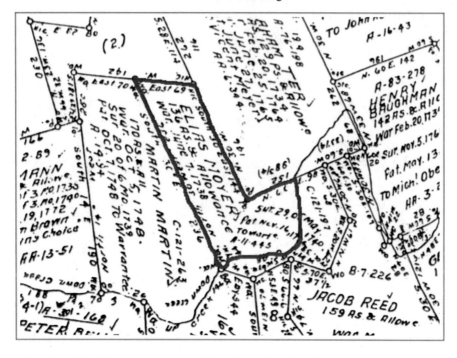

A section of the Warrant map showing Elias Meyer's land (written as Moyer here and the neighboring properties, 1744.

listed as a miller and perhaps was indentured to a miller; after all, his father was a miller.

In a day and age where we have GPS and Satellite imagery, the survey of the Elias Meyer's land tract is fascinating. It lays out the boundaries as follows:

> Begining (sic) at a White Oak Corner of Jacob Read thence South 30 degrees East by said Read 68 perches to a White Oak, thence South 20 degrees West 62 perches to a White Oak, thence West by North by Vact(ant) Land 38 perches to a Black Oak. Thence South West by West 48 perches to a White Oak, cor. of Jacob Bowman's Land, thence West by North by 0 degrees. 44 perch to a White Oak. Thence North 30 degrees West by Christopher Solinger 236 perches to a White Oak. Thence East

> by Jacob Brotherly 69 perches to a Hickory,
> thence South 30 degrees East Abraham Terr 144
> perches to a post, thence N. 60 degrees East by
> 0 degrees. 98 perches to the place of begining
> (sic). Containing one hundred and thirty seven
> acres."[15]

It is doubtful any of these trees or posts still exist. By the way, 1
perch equals 1/160th of an acre or 16.5 feet.

The Farmersville Mill

Being already established in Lancaster County gave Elias
an advantage that many settlers did not have. Most settlers right
off the boat would have experienced something like this:

> Then they had to travel into southeastern
> Pennsylvania by wagon and foot over unpaved
> roads/trails/riverbeds, not having much of an
> idea at all about what dangers might face
> them during the journey. There were no trains
> or steamships in those days along their path, so
> they had to rely on wagons and their feet.
> When they had to cross large rivers, there may
> have been a ferry they could use, but the small
> rivers they had to ford with their wagons.
> Somewhere along the way they had to buy
> their livestock -- cattle, pigs, chickens, goats,
> and take them along with them on their
> journey.[16]

Once they arrived at their warrant of land, they were met by trees
and large boulders. They would have to clear land to farm, cut
trees to build houses and barns, and find water to drink. Initially,
they would have lived out of the wagons or perhaps in a quickly
constructed lean-to.

However, by the time Elias received his warrant, his family
was formed and established in Earl Township. This meant that

while construction on his mill and home were being completed, he likely had adequate shelter, at least according to 1740s standards.

When the winter of 1741 hit, this was important. January that year received more than three feet of snow. Settlers in the remote parts of Lancaster ran out of bread and had to live off wildlife they found dead near the creeks and swamps near their houses. Many horses and cattle also died. In a farm that had only two horse or two head of cattle, this was an immense loss. Indians in the area feared that the loss of deer and turkeys during this season would be felt for years to come.[17]

While we do not know exactly when Elias Meyer built his mill, we know it existed by 1750 when it first appears on Earl Township tax records. It became known by the locals as the Farmersville Mill.[18] He built a grist mill, which, though the name technically means "Corn Mill", ground all sorts of grain into flour. Local farmers like his neighbors Jacob Read, Christopher Salinger, Jacob Brotherly, and Abraham Herr (Terr on the Warrant map above) would bring their own grain to be ground and received back meal or flour, minus a percentage called "the miller's toll." His mill would have been crucial since bread would have been a staple in the early settlers' diet.[19]

His 34 by 46 foot mill had an attached water-house that measured 34 by 22 feet.[20] He built a log dam that diverted water from the Conestoga River and powered the mill. He and his sons, along with other help he might have hired, dug a 125 foot channel, called a head race; this carried water from the dam to the wheel-house. In the wheelhouse, he installed a vertically mounted water wheel. He also dug a 100 foot channel coming out of the mill, called a tail race, that allowed the water to flow back into the Conestoga. Water flowing through here allowed the waterwheel to spin which in turn spun the pit wheel (mounted on the same axel as the water wheel) and likewise drove a smaller gear-wheel called the wallower. The wallower was mounted on the main driveshaft which turned the mill stones.

A Photo of Elias Meyer's house, the Miller's House, in the 1920s - 1940s

Although Elias Jr. eventually installed rollers, his father initially installed mill stones to grind grain. The bottom stone, called the bed stone, was fixed to the floor of the mill while the top stone, called a runner stone, was mounted on a separate spindle driven by the main shaft. A wheel called a stone nut connected the runner's spindle to the main drive shaft and could be disconnected, causing the runner to stop spinning. In this case, the main drive shaft could be used to drive a mechanical sieve to refine flour or to wind a chain to hoist up bags of grain. The distance between the stones could be adjusted to produce the grade of flour required. The closer the stones, the finer the flour.[21]

One can imagine for a moment, Elias standing on the top floor of the mill, yelling down to his sons as they lugged the sacks of grain onto the platform where they waited to be hoisted to the top of the mill. Once loaded, Elias released the mechanism activating the wheel driven hoist. At the top he, perhaps with his sons who may have ridden the hoisted platform to the top, carried the sacks inside and emptied them into bins, where the grain would work its way from the hopper to the millstones below. The

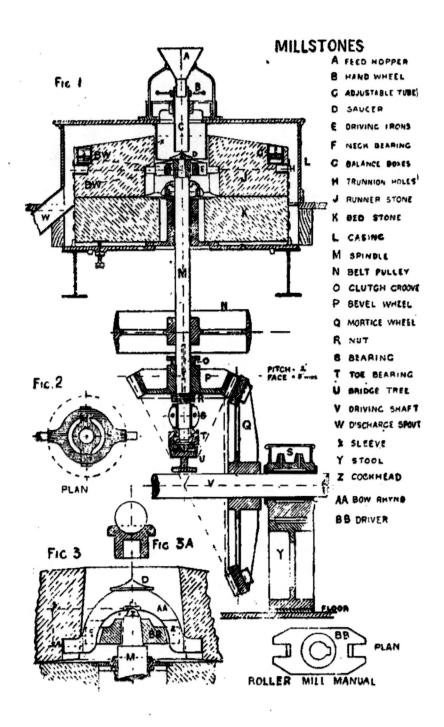

MILLSTONES

- **A** FEED HOPPER
- **B** HAND WHEEL
- **C** ADJUSTABLE TUBE)
- **D** SAUCER
- **E** DRIVING IRONS
- **F** NECK BEARING
- **G** BALANCE BOXES
- **H** TRUNNION HOLES
- **J** RUNNER STONE
- **K** BED STONE
- **L** CASING
- **M** SPINDLE
- **N** BELT PULLEY
- **O** CLUTCH GROOVE
- **P** BEVEL WHEEL
- **Q** MORTICE WHEEL
- **R** NUT
- **S** BEARING
- **T** TOE BEARING
- **U** BRIDGE TREE
- **V** DRIVING SHAFT
- **W** DISCHARGE SPOUT
- **X** SLEEVE
- **Y** STOOL
- **Z** COCKHEAD
- **AA** BOW RHYND
- **BB** DRIVER

Fig 1

Fig. 2

PLAN

PITCH = 1'
FACE = 5" WIDE

Fig 3

Fig 3A

FLOOR

PLAN

ROLLER MILL MANUAL

34

flow of grain was regulated by shaking it into a trough known as a slipper from which it would fall into a hole in the center of the running stone. After the milled grain worked its way through the grooves in the runner stone, it traveled down a chute and was collected in a sack on the ground or meal floor.[22]

In the early 1800s after Elias Junior took over the mill, he converted the mill stones to a roller system, and installed five double stands of 18 rollers in the mill for grinding wheat. The rollers were 24 inches in diameter and 25 feet long and used a bolting system with three bolting chests. The bolting cloth used to sift the flour came from Switzerland and was woven with a 120 mesh per square inch. The bolting reels were made by Washington Fry, a millwright in Ephrata, PA, widely known for his skillful work. This mill was one of the first to install the roller system for grinding flour.[23] The mill produced the following brands: Look Out, King of All, White Rose, and R and B.[24]

We will return to Elias Meyer in a few pages.

The Bird-in-Hand/Seven Day Baptist Trail

Perhaps another reason Elias built the mill where he did was that the Bird-in-Hand trail crossed the Conestoga Creek below the foot of the mill's dam. This was the same trail referred to as the Seven Day Baptist Trail which ended at the village of Bird-in-Hand.[25] Before the era of roads, Elias most likely used this trail for commerce and travel.

The Mill Story After Elias

The mill that Elias Meyer built was damaged by a severe flood in 1850 and then demolished. A second mill was built by Isaac Burkholder using northern Pennsylvania white pine. The dam was also rebuilt since it too had been destroyed. The mill again was destroyed in a severe flood in 1869. In 1872 Isaac Burkholder sold it to Joseph W. Rupp, his brother-in-law. Issac

The house that Joseph Rupp moved into. Built by John Rupp, it sits behind the miller's house.

was married to Joseph's sister Maria. Joseph rebuilt the mill for a third time.

In 1908, the first of two tragedies struck Joseph Rupp. Joseph was both a farmer and a miller. One morning Joseph loaded a wagon with manure and drove his two horse team out across a field to fertilize it. The wagon hit a rut and "a sudden jolt threw him under the wheels."[26] The horse team pulling wagon did not stop. They had carried out this routine many times before. The wagon, loaded down with manure, ran over his back.

Though no bones were broken, physicians worried the injuries might prove fatal. The weight of a wagon laden with manure could have done some serious damage. However, he made a full recovery.

But this may have been his deciding factor to hand the mill and its operations over to his sons. His sons, Samuel and David, took over operation of the mill in 1910. Joseph moved into the house next door. In 1918, a second tragedy struck Joseph.

Murder Near The Hertzog Homestead

By this time, Joseph was known in Lancaster County as a notable tobacconist and farmer. During the middle of the winter in 1918, he was stripping tobacco in his barn's tobacco cellar. He was processing the plant by removing leaves from the stalks which had hung in the barn drying and curing from fall into winter. After leaves were stripped, they were then baled.

On February 8th, on Friday afternoon at 4 o'clock, a 57 year old day laborer by the name of Adam Henry was helping Joseph with this chore. Earlier that day, Joseph had displayed a large amount of money while the two were alone. Everything seemed to be going well; they chatted about the day, perhaps about Great War being fought overseas, with no hint of animosity between them. When Joseph turned to pick up tobacco stalk from the floor, Adam whacked him over the head with a lead pipe.

Adam left Joseph for dead and went to the farmhouse where he attacked Harriet Schaeffer Rupp, Joseph's 80 year old wife. Thinking he had incapacitated her, he climbed the stairs to the second floor and found $35 dollars in Joseph's wallet. Meanwhile, Mrs. Rupp managed to reach the telephone and tried to call for help. Adam descended the stairs and discovered her in the act; he tore the phone out of the wall, and then left at a run.

Immediately, Harriet ran to a neighboring farm and pleaded for help. Several of the farm laborers mounted horses and scoured the surrounding farmland. Though the winter fields provided no cover, plenty of trees still forested the countryside. The cold winter that year, with temperatures plummeting to -4 degrees Fahrenheit and snowfall reaching 42 inches, meant that it was only a matter of time until Adam was apprehended.

After an hour's search, Clayton Sweigart caught Adam Henry getting ready to board a trolley at Metzler's Station, about a mile away from the Rupp house and next door to the Hertzog Homestead. He handed him over to Chief of Police J. W. Werner.[27] [28]

Three weeks later when some of the snow had melted, Joseph Rupp's pocketbook was found behind the tobacco shed on Frank Adams' farm with the three $10 dollar bills and one $2 dollar bills still in it. Adam had tossed it there while being pursued by Sweigert.

Joseph lived for another month, but due to his advanced age and the injuries sustained from the pipe, he died early Monday morning on March 11, 1918. Dr. Walter of Brownstown testified at a hearing that Joseph's death was the direct result of the blow to his head, and Adam Henry went on to face a murder charge. He threatened to take his life and was put under guard.

On September 11, 1918, the case went to trial. Adam was found guilty of second degree murder.[29] In the years that followed, he tried to appeal this verdict twice: once in March of 1925[30] and

The Elias Meyer miller's house as it exists today.

A postcard of Conestoga Valley Park; the rollerskating rink and dance hall can be seen in the center.

then in September 1927.[31] He would have been in his late sixties by this point and most likely died in prison.

This was not the first time Adam tangled with the law. He had served jail time a year earlier for stealing a team of horses in East Petersburg, PA.[32]

Frivolity at Conestoga Valley Park

But the land near the mill was not just filled with tragedy. The mill was located near what was known as Conestoga Park, now know as Conestoga Campground, home to a selection of summer and year round cottages. During its days as a park, dances and roller skating were featured there. On the land between the park and the mill during the time between the turn of the century to World War I, families would spend vacations and even their entire summers camping and fishing along the Conestoga.[33]

Rupp's Mill in disrepair sometime in the late 1960's. Photo and information from "Through the Years: Photographic Views of the Cocalico Valley" by Cynthia Marquet

The demolition of the Rupp's Mill in 1976 from my father's collection.

The mill remained in the family until 1973. In the years that followed, it rapidly changed hands. Samuel L. and Mariam Martin purchased the property in 1973. They divided up the mill property and sold it in lots. The main structures were sold in 1975 to Leon and Edna Horning. They tore down mill in 1976. No mill exists on the current property.[34] The miller's house and the land where the mill stood was purchased by Wilmer and Deborah Weaver in 1978, who live on the property until this day.

This building dedicated 1847.

Muddy Creek Lutheran Church

One thing that still exists is Elias Meyer's house. It most likely was constructed after the mill, perhaps sometime in the late 1750s. According to Thomas Weaver, the aforementioned school teacher who lived on the property, there was a date stone on the house at one time, but when the family sand-blasted the whitewash off the house, the writing on the date stone became unrecognizable.

From Father to Sons

On December 28, 1752, Elias purchased an additional 64 acres from Emanuel Harman (who had originally bought the acreage from Martin Martin), giving him a total of 200 acres. It seems clear by his actions 8 years later that he was considering the future and thinking about retirement. This land was part of Peter and Elias Junior's inheritance. By this time, his other sons, Vincent and John, already had their own farms.

In 1753 he appears as one of three deacons in the Bergstrasse Lutheran Church, in Earl township. As mentioned, his children were baptized at the Muddy Creek Lutheran Church. While perhaps I earlier implied Elias was Anabaptist, this does not seem to be the case, at least not in America; however, the conditions of the political landscape that impacted the Anabaptists would have affected him as well. Johann Wilhelm who took over after the death of Karl Ludwig was a devote Catholic and had no grace for the Protestant Reformation. Elias Meyer's exodus from the Palatinate as a Lutheran coincided with the Swiss Mennonites, and he and his family traveled with them on their ships.

A 1794 Coin found around the Elias Meyer home.

Louisa died on February 6, 1759 and was buried in the Cocalico Reformed Graveyard, near Ephrata, PA. By November 1760, Elias married his second wife Barbara. She died before December of 1761. Soon after, he married his third wife Maria Elizabeth Gardner.

On November 27th, 1760, Elias and Barbara deeded off the northern 100 acres in Earl Township to their son Peter.[35] The northern part of this is the current tract of land on which the Hertzog Homestead sits. This deed describes the several tracts of land together with all singular houses, outhouses, edifices and buildings, thereon erected and built. This sort of terminology appears on most early deeds, or indentures as they were called, and did not suggest that there were actual buildings on the property. There might have been; we just can not be sure.

The several tracts of land perhaps is a reference to the fact that Elias Meyer originally owned part of this land and the other part was owned by Martin Martin. Martin sold it to Emanuel Harmon, and Emanuel, along with his wife Anna Marie, sold it to Elias as previously mentioned. So Peter's land was comprised of

Louisa Meyer's Tombstone

the 36 acres that originally belonged to Elias and 64 that originally belonged to Martin Martin.

Another interesting thing about Peter's land is that it borders the land of Jacob Brotherly, Abraham Herr, Martin Brown, and John Meyer, his older brother, who apparently had land next to Peter's. Vincent, his other brother who was married to Ann, witnessed the deed between Elias Senior and Peter.

On December 10th, 1761, Elias Junior received the remaining 100 acres originally belonging to Elias, land which adjoined Peter Meyer's, the late Abraham Herr's and the late Jacob Reed's. He took over his father's mill.[36]

Elias died somewhere between 1762 and 1766 and was buried in the Cocalico Reformed Graveyard.[37][38]

How This Impacted the Hertzog Homestead

The earliest piece of the land, 136 acres, that would eventually become the Hertzog Homestead was deeded to Elias Meyer as a warrant in 1738 and officially granted to him in 1744. In 1752 he purchased an additional 64 acres from his neighbor Emanuel Harman. The land on which the Hertzog Homestead sits was made up of these 64 acres and an additional 36 acres that were part of Elias' original warrant.

The Elias Meyer Family Tree

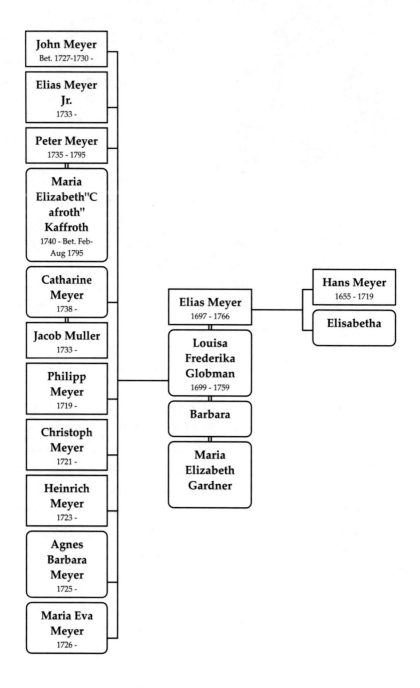

Peter Meyer
The Beginnings of the Hertzog Homestead

Clearing the Land

Peter stood, sweat trickling down his brow and his axe propped against his trousers, staring out over an acre of land that he and his brothers had spent the summer clearing. Stumps still dotted the edges of the field, hemmed in by the the tall oaks, chestnuts, and hickory. Many of these trees had helped build the barn and his small log house that stood nearby; many stones and rocks had been pulled from the fields to wall up the sides of the barn. It was backbreaking and arduous work.

The late afternoon sun dipped below the tops of the trees as his picked up the axe and ambled toward home, where his wife Maria and his four children were waiting.

Peter Meyer's Early Years

Peter Meyer, also known as Johan Peter Meyer, was the sixth of ten sons born to Elias and Louisa. He was born in Lancaster, PA on June 13, 1735 and was baptized at Muddy Creek Lutheran Church at the age of 10 months, early the following year. [1]

Not much is known about Peter's growing up and formative years. By the time he was nine, his father received a warrant for the land around the Conestoga River, and it seems likely that he, along with his three brothers and his father's neighbors, helped clear the land and build the mill.

The year 1759 brought grief and joy to Peter. In February his mother died. Soon after this, Peter fell in love with Maria Elizabeth Koffroth and then married her on November 13, 1759 at the Cocalico Reformed Church. Maria, the daughter of Gerhard and Maria Barbara Koffroth, was born on October 24, 1740 and was baptized at the Cocalico Reformed Church.[2]

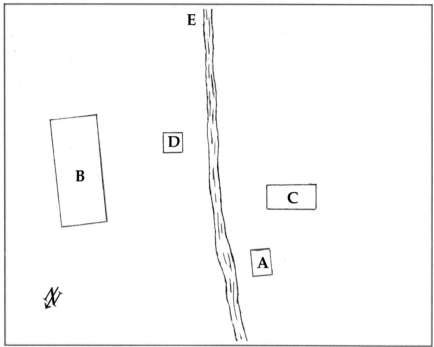

A. The 13 X 16 foot log house built around 1760   B. The 30 X 65 foot Sweitzer Barn built around 1765 C. The 15 X 30 foot stone house built around 1770 - cellar entrance to east; first floor entrance to west D. The carriage house built in the 1770s E. Stream emptied into the Conestoga River about ¾ mile away, 100 yards down stream from Elias Meyer's mill.

Building the Jacob Metzler Plantation

On November 27, 1760, almost a year after Peter   was married, he inherited the northern 100 acres of Elias Meyer's land. [3] The Hertzog Homestead stands in what was once the middle of this tract of land. As previously mentioned, this land included 34 acres from Elias Meyer's original warrant and 66 acres that was originally warranted to Martin Martin.

There is no further mention of Peter and no indication as to what is going on with his property until the 1769 Tax Records. However, based on records from the establishment of other properties in the area, we can draw some conclusions about those nine years.

What the Peter Moyer log house may have looked like.

He was married a little over a year when he acquired the deed to the property. Most likely he and his new bride continued living at home with his father Elias. We do not know when Peter, Elias Junior, and Elias exactly began talking about splitting the 200 acres, but we do know that a year after Peter married, he received the upper 100 acres of the plantation; a little over a year later, on December 10, 1761, Elias Junior inherits over the lower 100 acres with the grist mill; and within the next four years Elias Meyer dies. Peter probably did not live for long at the Elias Meyer house after these events, especially since his first

What the interior of Peter's log house may have looked like.

child was born later that year. However, his time living in his father's house gave him the time he needed to build the log house and the barn on his new land.

The Log House

One of the first things he built was the log house. He constructed this with the help of his neighbors, his father, and brothers. The log house originally had a dirt floor and no windows, though both those items were probably added later on. Peter certainly had the tools to build it, having at his death instruments such as three axes, a hammer and two pinchers, two chisels, three files, two augers, three gimblebs, a hand saw, a square, a cross cut saw, a crow bar, and so forth.[4]

Jacob N. Metzler, who eventually bought the property from Peter, mentions the log house in his will where he tells the executors of his will that his wife needs to be provided "such articles yearly as grain, wood house, and stable." There is no indication that Jacob Metzler built the log house as some have speculated, but rather that he was granting provision for her use of an existing building.

This log house also appears in a book on the Metzler Mennonite Church history edited by David Sauder. It states Noah Mack, a school teacher and preacher, and his new wife, Elizabeth, lived in this log house soon after they were married in 1882. It states that "they started housekeeping in the Spring of 1883 in an old log house on the premises of Jacob Metzler."[5]

A sketched picture of Noah Mack who lived in the Peter Meyer log house.

The log house was located across the street from where the Hertzog Homestead house now exists. We know this because at one point while the Reuben Oberholtzer was

50

plowing his garden (this was land that once belonged to Peter) they found foundation stones for the log house.

Other evidence for the existence of this log house exists on insurance documents from Mennonite Mutual Aide for Jacob S. Metzler, the grandson of Jacob N. Metzler, who also eventually owned the property. The document references a building called the "summer house," measuring 16 by 13 feet on 1888-1890 insurance documents. In 1888 this building was included with the property of the stone dwelling house on the Hertzog Homestead; then a year later he seems to reconsider which insurance policy to attach it to and includes it with the two story frame dwelling house, which later became his widow and unmarried daughter's house. This summer house was clearly a building separate from the two story dwelling house and its attachments. It seems clear that this was the log house and that it existed into the late 1800s.

One will also note the Noah Mack refers to it as the "Old Log House." While what constitutes something as old can be a bit ambivalent, it suggests that when Noah Mack occupied the house, it had been around a long time.

Though considered a more temporary shelter, this log house would have given Peter and his wife shelter from the elements. Given its 13 by 16 foot size, it was most likely divided into two rooms: a kitchen and a stove room. Early settlers many times slept on the floor.[6]

The Sweitzer Barn

After Peter finished the log home, Peter began construction on his barn, emphasizing the priority he placed on agriculture. By 1770, he had two horses, one cow, and four sheep. While some settlers allowed their animals to roam free, it is quite possible the barn was constructed by this time to shelter such animals.

Most, if not all the land Peter received was "unimproved" land, meaning that it could not be farmed. By 1770, some 30 acres had been cleared or improved. Part of these unknown years were

The Peter Meyer barn shown with some additions 2013

The north gable wall with ventilation slits

likely spent clearing the land of trees and boulders with the help of his neighbors, so that he could work and plant the land.

In 1770 and 1771 Earl Township records show Peter as being charged a "Quit-Rent." Elias Meyer probably paid this as well; it was just not recorded. William Penn and his sons imposed a quit-rent as an initial charge of living on the soil. It was a relic of feudalism and emphasized that the colonies were subservient to the British crown. In a sense it was saying that Peter Meyer did not really own his land, but that the Penn's did. The Quit-Rent fee Peter paid was ½ penny per acre.[7]

The back of the Peter Meyer barn shown with some additions. Photo courtesy of Dale Ebersole.

The 1815 tax records refer to a stone barn measuring 65 feet by 30 feet; the main barn today still measures this. In 1783 it is first mentioned on tax records. That makes it the oldest building the property still in existence, most likely predating the Revolutionary War. There is a date in the barn, but from tax records it is clear this was not the date it was built. 1813 appears in plaster inside the the upper north gable of the barn. The DP most likely refers to "Date Plastered" though these could be someone's initials. Certainly no one living on the farm at this time had said initials.

The barn that Peter built was a Classic-Sweitzer Barn, a type of barn that began appearing in the area around the 1750s. The fact that these were called Sweitzer barns indicates their Swiss origins. These types of barns existed in Switzerland long before the settlers arrived in America.

The barn has three limestone sides with a stone stable wall in the front. This stone was quarried form the field by Peter Meyer with the help of Elias Jr. and the help of neighbors. In an inventory list after Peter's death, it lists a "Sam(sic) Stone pick and hammer and instrument". This certainly suggests he had the means to do the quarrying himself. The upper part of the north gable wall was

A slat form the granary stenciled with Jacob Metzler's name circa the late 1700s. The date below, the only date on the barn, indicates the year it was plastered, right after Jacob Metzler's death.

ventilated with vertical slits in the limestone. The south upper gable wall most likely mimicked this, but it was torn down to the top of the first level in order to extend the length of the barn in the 1840s during Lancaster County's agricultural boom.

The second floor of the barn has two large hay mows on either side of the double threshing floor. Heavy bents of hewn oak, mortise-and-tenonned and pinned, provide the inner support for the barn and roof. Bents were a cross-section of the timber

Above the entrance to the granary; to the right, the four bays in the granary are clearly evident.

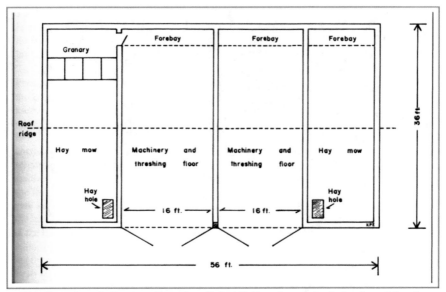

This floor plan of a Sweitzer Barn from Robert F. Ensminger's book closely matches the Peter Meyer barn

frame that supported the trestles. The bents were located on either side of the double threshing floor.

The front of the threshing bays contain a sliding rolling door, probably originally a hinged door, that Peter would have used to provide a draft for hand threshing and winnowing. This also would have allowed straw and hay to be tossed into the barnyard below.

The forebay of the barn provided Peter Meyer a place to store straw, grain, bags, and fodder on the ground floor and out of the weather. The seven foot overhang helped to keep snow from blocking the stable

The forebay of the barn.

Wood shingling dating back to the 18th century

doors and also helped keep the rain from eroding the barn's foundation. Like other Sweitzer barns, it has a heavy plank stairway leading up from the front stable into the forebay above. Heavy beams support the forebay and jut back over the front stable wall, continuing over the summer beam and into the back wall. Some of these beams just reach back to the summer beam. The summer beam is the central beam that runs the length of the barn and supports the forebay beams and the second floor.

Like many Sweitzer barns, the granary was built over the forebay, at the front left side of the threshing floor, with a door that provided access to the granary from the threshing floor. The granary was located on the southern end of the barn allowing it to get the most sun for best drying. That it is located over the forebay only assisted in the drying process. The four bins in the granary allowed it to store va variety of grain.

The floor plan from Robert F. Ensminger's book mirrors the upper floor of Meyer's barn (see page 55), the exception being the hay hole on the right is actually flipped onto the edge of the threshing floor. There is also a hay hole that was added later near the middle of the barn beside the center wall of the threshing floor. The Meyer barn is 33 feet wide and 65 feet long.[8]

The barn was originally shingled in wood, some of which can still be seen under the tin roof that exists today. What it must have looked like in the 18th century is evident on a portion of corn crib that was sheltered under a later addition to the barn.

How Old is the Stone House?

According to 1815 District Tax records, a one story house built of stone and wood 30 feet in length and 15 feet deep existed on the plantation. As previously suggested, it most likely was not the first house. According to Kutztown Professor Robert F. Ensminger, an expert in Pennsylvania farms, by the 1750s "German Farmers were already building large barns, while retaining modest log dwellings."[9] The barn was typically built before a more permanent dwelling was established.

The 1783 tax records describe a dwelling. Was this dwelling the log house on the property or something else? Did Peter use the 13 by 16 foot log home to shelter his family? While we cannot be absolutely certain of this, we can perhaps speculate a little bit.

In the years after Peter took ownership the property, his family grew rapidly. Conrad was born September 29, 1761, Regina was born between 1762-1764, Mathias was born December 11, 1765, Frederick and Henry were born between 1766 and 1770, Davis was born on October 29, 1771, Christina was born between 1772 and 1775, Peter was born in 1776 and later becomes a miller, Elizabeth was born in 1779, and Adam completed the family being

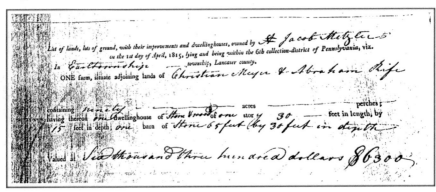

1815 District Tax Records

One can see a district rock line that starts where the sandstone stops and travels across the top of the first window and then stops and comes down a few feet before the second window.

born in 1781. With this size family, a family of 12, it seems unlikely, though not impossible, that the log house continued to function as the main dwelling house mentioned in the 1783 tax records. It is more likely the house described in the 1815 tax records.

One quandary is that only one house is mentioned on the 1783 tax records. The term used in the records is "dwelling house." This basically meant a house which was occupied and lived in; it leaves room for the log house to be in existence, but since it was not lived in or a primary residence, it would not be counted as the dwelling house. Another probable scenario is that in law terms, a dwelling house includes a "group of buildings, occupied by a family as a place of residence." In that case, Peter and Maria could have been living in both

1985 Photo shows the Northwest corner

the 30 by 15 stone house and the 13 by 16 log house.

A More Permanent Dwelling

So what did Peter Meyer's second dwelling look like? When Jacob H. Metzler converted this one story dwelling into a 2 story plantation house, he did not tear down the original stone dwelling, but in fact incorporated into the new structure. Because of this, we know more about how Peter's house was laid out.

We know that Jacob H. Metzler did not raze the original stone house for a couple of reasons. First, Jacob's house has sand stone corners that rise from the bottom of the first story to the top of the second story except for the northwest corner, in which the sandstone only comes down to the top of the first floor. Second, mortar lines on the west side of the house also suggest the original walls were incorporated into the current house. There is a distinct line in the mortar at the top of the first floor level that travels from the northern corner to toward the southern corner and ends half way between at what looks like might have been a window or door.

There is further evidence in the floor in the north western corner of the house. The basement and the first floor contains a layer of wood, a layer of rye straw (which was bitter to rodents) and mud, and then another layer of wood. None of the other flooring on the first floor has this. It was suggested by the Lancaster's Historic Preservation Society that this might have been used for insulation or as fire prevention. The section is right above the lowest and dampest part of the cellar, the location of the original root cellar. In the book *Architecture and Landscape of the Pennsylvania Germans, 1720 - 1920*, Sally McMurry writes, "this helped keep the cellar at an even temperature for food storage and processing" (35).[10] It would have kept the upper floor from being damp and cold as well.

The house faced south with its back toward the current road. The house was built into a bank of a hill, which helped keep

Barring some stylistic differences, Peter Meyer's house would have look in shape like the Hans Herr house, which was built early in the 18th century. Note the way the right side backs up to a bank.

the root cellar underneath cool in the summer and from freezing in the winter.

Cellar access was most likely from the eastern side. He used this cellar to store cider in both fermented and unfermented forms, as well as keep butter, cabbages, milk, and vinegar. Two narrow small windows in the northern most stone wall allowed air to move through the cellar, prevented both dampness and mold. During the winter month straw was placed in front of these to prevent the freezing of food. This is a practice we have continued up till this day, although instead of being concerned about food freezing, we are more concerned about pipes.

The forest surrounding the farmstead provided wood for the roof shingles and interior partitions. His crosscut saw, hand saw, square, and other implements for shaping the beams and roof

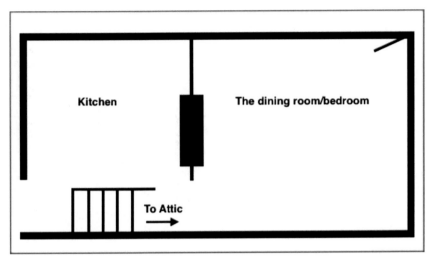

The floor plan of Peter Meyer's flur küchenhaus

served him and his neighbors well as they cleared the land and used the wood to build this house. The floor was laid with Pennsylvania Pine. He even had chisels and files for creating the mortising holes and tenons which connected the beams.

The main floor of the house was split into two rooms with a fireplace and chimney in the middle that helped heat both rooms. The eastern room   functioned as a living room family, room and dining room. The was referred to as the "stube" or stove room. Peter and Maria slept here as well since it was near the fireplace. It contained what is sometimes called a "cult-corner". We often referred to this as a Bible closet. Peter kept his large Bible and his other books and might have kept his pewter there as well.[11]

Although he had a family of 12, in today's world we might find it a bit odd that he had a table, but only three chairs. Most early settlers used benches since they could easily and inexpensively make from hardwoods surrounding the farm. Typical houses like this one would have had "a table in the corner with benches fastened to the wall."[12] This area would have been used for eating and various other work activities.

The kitchen was most likely in the western room. If there was cellar access, it was from this room. Food was cooked over the raised hearth that stood between the two rooms, most likely in the cooper kettle that Maria used.

Evidence on interior wall of the kitchen indicates stairs led up to the attic from this room. The stairs most likely wound at a right angle with no landing. This attic would have provided Peter's

The German Bible closet/cult-corner.
Photo by Sierra Thomas.

family with the additional sleeping area they needed. Many times children slept in the attic. They would sleep three or four to a bed. Peter placed a six plate stove to help heat the attic. Still, for the children sleeping up there in the cold winter months, they would have needed blankets layered upon blankets, for the wood shingled roof, while protecting them from rain, would have let in the blustery winter wind and the blowing snow.

Entrance into the house, as indicated in the stonework, was on the western end of the house through the kitchen. This type of house was called a flur küchenhaus or corridor-kitchen house.[13] If there was a third room, of which some early homesteads had, it was the bed room. Peter is recorded as having an old bed-stead, suggesting this might be the case.

A Steward of the Land

After the barn building was completed, Peter continued to improve his land. By 1771 he had 40 acres of improved land. How much he improved by the time Jacob N. Metzler bought the farm is unclear. Tax records show that by the late 1800s there were only 20 acres of unimproved land left. But in the late 1700s, a typical farm of that time only had 35 acres that were improved for crops and buildings.[14] The rest was forested. Peter used a portion of this forty acres of cleared land for his barn and log house.

From the inventory list at Peter's death, we know that he grew wheat, flax, hemp, potatoes, and had an orchard on the farm. While the German settlers did not clear large amount of land, "that which they did use was cleared thoroughly. 'In destroying underwood and brushes...they generally grub them out of the ground, by which means, a field is fit for cultivation the second year after it is cleared, as it is twenty years afterwards.'"[15]

Peter gave careful attention to the land. Like many of the settlers before him, he fertilized his fields and gardens with manure. Many settlers also used lime to assist in a fields water absorption and and improve a plant's intake of nutrients. "In 1754 Thomas Pownall observed that 'every farmer has a limekiln for the dressing of his land.'"[16] The remains of Peter's limekiln can still be seen on the property today and will be discussed later. It was this care of the land and that of the other Lancaster farmers that helped Lancaster become known as Pennsylvania's garden spot.

After Peter brought in his harvest, what he did not use for personal living, he took to his brother's mill to be ground and bagged. It was then shipped off to market. At home his wife Maria would have mixed rye with wheat for baking a "middlin bread." While this initially meant a dark loaf whose bran had been removed, it suggested a bread of superior quality. He would have used his flax for linen, the preferred clothing of the early German settlers; he also had sheep which suggested he also used wool. Any corn he raised would have been fed to the livestock since it was considered unfit for humans. And he used hemp was used for rope, bed ticking, and grain bags.

Animals were typically allowed to roam free, and while they had meadows set aside for them, they often foraged the unimproved land. Peter also used the meadow to harvest hay for

A replica of the Pennsylvania long rifle - made by Wilmer Weaver

feeding animals in the winter. Fields and gardens were often fenced to keep animals out rather then fence them in. From Earl Township Tax records, we have a good idea of what sort of livestock he had. For the most part he always owned two horses, had one to three horned cattle, and four to seven sheep. With many current farms in Lancaster, PA containing fifty head of cattle or more, one might wonder why Peter (as mentioned in 1783 Tax records) did not have more in the way of livestock to help feed the family? Perhaps it was that the principal flesh food for families was found in deer and turkey from the surrounding forests.[17] So instead of using cattle for food, they were generally used to plow fields. Horses were expensive.

At his death, Peter owned a red cow, a black cow, and a spotted cow, which he used to make butter in the cask and butter tub he owned. He also owned a Rone(sic) mare. He had 8 geese, 2 sheep (which he sheared), and 6 hogs, which he would have slaughtered and turned into pork and sausage, using his sausage funnel.[18]

Peter built his barn and dwelling in its current location due to a steam that flowed between the two. The stream eventually emptied into the Conestoga River. This stream bed is now dry only runs with water when it rains. At one time springs from the hill to the north, now crowned by the town of Akron, provided an ample source of drinkable water. It would have run behind the log house giving Peter and his wife easy access to water.

This stream would have also attracted wildlife, which Peter would have used to supplement his family's diet. The woods were filled with deer, wild turkey, rabbits, quail, and pheasants. Most farmers owned guns; this is one of the reasons that the Pennsylvania long rifle was first produced in Lancaster County. My great uncle Martin Mylin is credited with birthing the Pennsylvania long rifle, though some historians think its was more likely his son who was the gunsmith. It is possible that Peter may have used one of his guns; he had a gun and the gears to it.[19]

Inventory lists of the Metzlers, who lived on the property after Peter, indicate that the farm had orchards. Most likely, the initial orchard would have been laid out by Peter. Typically orchards ranged from 50 to 100 trees; primarily these were apples such as Romanites, Hoop's, Ramboe's, Newton Pippen, English russets, Hay's apple, English codlin, sweet early, tart early, sweet winter, lacker, spice apple, clempsonites, catheat, Spitzenberg, and others.[20] Peter's family ate these fresh, stored them in cellars over the winter, dried them for eating and cooking, made them into apple butter, and served them to livestock. However, apple cider was the core use; German settlers consumed this in huge quantities. They drank it fresh and fermented. At his death, Peter had an apple mill, along with 4 casks which suggested he raised apples, made cider and vinegar, something we know the Metzlers who followed him did as well.[21] He was a bee keeper and had around 8 bee hives for the production of honey. This also aided in the pollination of his orchards.

The Changing of the Guard

In 1786, Peter Meyer dropped off the Earl Township tax records and a German Mennonite Jacob Metz (a misspelling of Metzler on the tax records) a coverlet weaver, took over the farm. His name was spelled correctly on the deed. He shows up again on 1787 tax records, this time with the correct spelling of his name, Jacob Metzler, with his occupation again listed as a weaver.

Why did Peter sell the farm and the land deeded to him by his father? Perhaps the few records of him after he left clue us in.

On June 19, 1786, Peter bought land in Codorus Township, York County from Caspar Reinecker and his wife Anna Maria. John Meyer, Peter's brother, acted as an intermediary in the sale. In 1789, Codorus Township records list him as owning 400 acres, 3 horses, 3 cattle, and a sawmill. In 1790, the census shows his entire family was still living with him.

His move off his original farm seems to be out of a desire to provide land for his son. The 100 acres he lived on would hardly have sufficed as an inheritance for his sons. By 1792, Peter began to sell his land, dividing it between his sons Frederick, Mathias, and Conrad. Peter first sold twenty acres, still retaining 380 acres and the sawmill. This drops to 300 acres in 1793, but again he still owned the sawmill and apparently a waterworks. 80 acres were sold to his son Mathais. Maria Elizabeth, Peter's wife, died somewhere between February and August of 1795. Peter died in August of 1795.[22]

Some of the Meyers remained in the area of Elias Meyer's warrant throughout the 18th and 19th centuries. Christian Meyer, Jr. appears on deeds, wills, and other documents. He served as a trustee when Metzler's Mennonite Church was first established. Another Daniel Meyer served as trustee from 1864 to 1890. In 1864, there were three Meyers or Myer farms that lay within the vicinity of the Hertzog Homestead.

How This Connects To The Hertzog Homestead

Peter Meyer formed the beginnings of what is the Hertzog Homestead. After he received the acreage from his father, he began the clearing of the land. Peter built the log house that stood on the property into the late 1800s. He also constructed the barn that still stands on the property today. A portion of the original western and northern walls as well as the floor of the one-story stone house he built has been incorporated into the two story plantation house as it exists today.

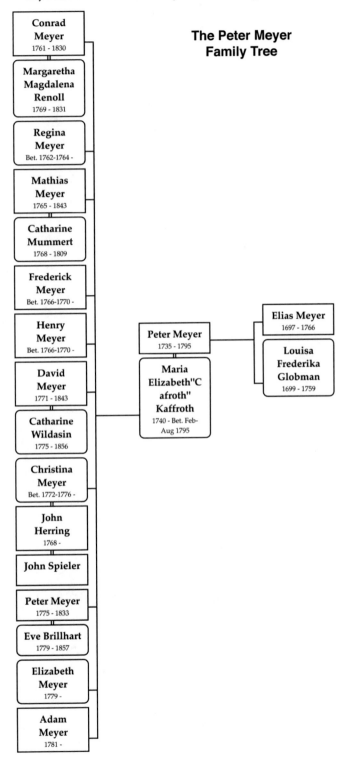

The Peter Meyer Family Tree

The Arrival of the Metzlers

K. Scott Hertzog

Thunder in the Valley

Valentine walked between the rows of corn that he had planted earlier in the spring. The air lay heavy, muggy, and hot as his fingers brushed the tops of the plants. Thunderheads roiled overhead; he was praying for rain. In his 27 years, he had never seen farming as terrible as the past three years. First it was the lack of rain; he had barely coaxed enough grain to feed his cattle and provide for his young family. He was thankful he had apprenticed as a coverlet weaver when he was orphaned. Without this skill, his family would have fallen on hard times.

And then, there was last year. The weather was so perfect and the crops were so bountiful he almost could not give away the wheat crop.

Now once again the spring had been dry. The corn was barely ankle high.

He smiled to himself. Dear Lord, I don't get to choose the weather. I trust in your provision.

The sky thundered. Valentine sprinted for the barn. As he ducked through a barn door, rain began to fall in torrents, a brisk cool wind whipping the drops against the barn.

And then hail began to fall, huge, the size of turkey eggs. Valentine stood frozen in horror. He pleaded, Oh Lord, make it stop. It continued to fall.

Metzlers in the Old World

Perhaps beginning in the old world prepared Valentine for hardships like that above. The story of Valentine Metzler, the father of Jacob Metzler who bought the plantation from Peter Meyer, begins in Windesheim, Germany. Windesheim is first mentioned in 1157 when Pope Eugene II had his possessions confirmed in the Abbey Deutz. The Catholic Church that stood there was demolished in 1517, but was later rebuilt. In 1550 the Catholic Church was converted in a Lutheran place of worship.

An artists depiction of Windesheim in the early 1600's. The church on the left is the 850 year old Evangelische Lutheran Kirche Windesheim.

Yost Metzler was born in 1693, a few years before Elias Meyer. His father, Johann Georg Metzler, was born around 1675 and possibly came from the Altenkirchen area of Germany. His mother's name is unknown. He grew up in a Lutheran family and had at least one brother, Johann Jacob Metzler, born in 1697. They were both baptized in Windesheim Parish Lutheran Church.

Some have suggested that Valentine was an Anabaptist. Many online records indicate that he came from Bollingen-Rapperswil, St.Gallen, Switzerland. However, the registrar for the church in Switzerland claims there were never any Metzler families in that area. The surname is unknown there. What is clear is that Yost and Valentine were Lutheran and were baptized in Windesheim Parish Lutheran Church.[1]

He married Anna Marie Schollenberger, also a Lutheran. She gave birth to Valentine on February 14/15, 1726, and he was baptized two days later in the same church his parents were. His other brothers and sisters were as follows:

> Catharina born on January 23, 1720; baptized on
> January 25, 1720.

Auszug aus dem Taufbuch

der Pfarrei Evangelisch-Lutherische Kirche   Jahrgang 1726

in   Windesheim Krs. Bad Kreuznach   Seite 85   lfd. Nr. –

Name des Täuflings: Johann Velten M E T Z L E R

Tag und Ort der Geburt: 15. Februar 1726 - Windesheim

Geschlecht: Männlich

Name des Vaters: Johann Jost M E T Z L E R

Konfession, Beruf: lutherisch, Beruf nicht angegeben

Name der Mutter: Anna Catharina M E T Z L E R (Geburtsname N.N.)

Konfession, Beruf: lutherisch - Hausfrau

Wohnort: Windesheim

Tag und Ort der Taufe: 17. Februar 1726 - Windesheim

Taufender Priester: N.N.   des Täuflings:

Taufpate (-zeuge): Johann Velten S C H M I D T   Konfession luth. ⟨Großvater mütterlicherseits

Taufpate (-zeuge): Anna Maria, Witwe von Philipp W I L H E L M   Konfession luth. ⟨Großmutter väterlicherseits

Bemerkungen:

Valentine Metzler's baptismal certificate - Courtesy of Nico Kittel

Anna Margaretha born on February 2, 1723; baptized on February 7, 1723

Johann Philipp born on January 5, 1729; baptized on January 9, 1729

Agnes born on April 19, 1732; baptized on April 21, 1732.[2]

Yost and Anna Marie faced many of the same struggles that Elias Meyer experienced. What forced the Meyer family to leave their homeland was most likely true for the Yost Metzler Family as well.

The name Metzler is Remish and comes from Rhiems, a city in northern France. Essentially, it meant butcher or provision dealer. The latin word is macellarius meaning provision dealer or macellium, meaning a provision or meat market.[3]

Evangelische Lutheran Kirche Windesheim dates back 850 years. Photo courtesy of Nico Kittel.

Metzlers in the New World

At the age 12, Valentine, along with his father Yost and his mother Anna, left from Rotterdam[4] and traveled to Cowes, England on the Ship Glasgow commanded by Walter Sterling. Eventually they landed in Philadelphia on September 9th, 1738. Yost was listed both as Joost Mitzlor and Joot Mittsler, age 45, on this Palatine boat. There were 120 men and 229 women and children on board. Since children under 16 are not listed by name on the ship's roster, it is not known whether Yost had other children traveling with him. What is known is that Yost died five years after arriving in 1743, leaving 17 year old Valentine an orphan. His mother died in childbirth to a sister that same year.

The Stehli Silk Mill

His sister Anna Maria survived. She might have been raised by her godparents who are listed on her mother's death certificate.[5]

Not much is known about Valentine's next five years. It is quiet probable that he became an Anabaptist during this time, under the decipleship of Jacob Nissley. He most likely worked on area farms as a laborer, perhaps helping clear land. Many orphans of that age did this, working as farm hands and traveling from farm to farm. Another possibility is that, since he later was listed as a coverlet weaver, perhaps he apprenticed with one. The second option seems to make more sense since he would have had to learn the skill.

Valentine Metzler Establishes his Farmstead

On November 19, 1749 at the age 23, Valentine married Anna Nissley. She was born in Switzerland on December 9, 1727 to Jacob Nissley of Rossmere. Valentine and Anna set up housekeeping on a farm several miles northeast of Lancaster, Pennsylvania, close to the point where the Pennsylvania Railroad crossed the Conestoga River. He was listed as being both a farmer

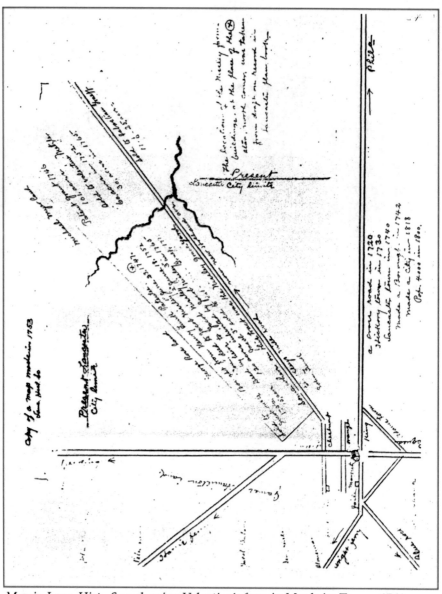

Map in Lanc. Hist., Soc. showing Valentine's farm in Manheim Twp. c. 1763

and a weaver[6]; this is important to note due to the aforementioned Jacob N. Metzler's apparent continuation of his father's weaving business. Jacob would have been 28 years old when his father passed away in 1783, suggesting he might have had his father's loom when he took over the Peter Meyer farm in 1786.

When Jacob Nissley died in 1752, his oldest son, Henry Nissley and his second oldest son, Jacob Nissley, refused to take the 211 acre Nissley place. After settlement by the orphan's court, they accepted the appraised price and sold sixty acres to their brother-in-law Valentine for 645 Pounds. This, together with the land he and Anna already owned, made a 90 acres farm east of Stehli Silk Mill and lands, now the eastern part of Lancaster City, PA.[7]

A Bad Time to Start Farming

According to the January 1968 Mennonite Research Journal and Lancaster County Pennsylvania: A History by H. M. J. Klien, Ph. D., these were terrible years to start farming. 1750 and 1751 experienced severe drought perhaps. Valentin's weaving helped his family survive during this years. Then in 1752 the harvest was so bountiful farmers could not sell their wheat; they fed it to the hogs instead. Then three years of drought followed. In Klien's book, Diffenderfer describes those years: "The earth was parched, and vegetation of all kinds perished for lack of moisture; a famine seemed impending." On June 17, 1763, a huge hailstorm, with hail as large as turkey eggs, fell decimating birds and small animals in large number and leaving trees "as destitute of foliage as in midwinter."[8]

The Indian Slaughter

Later that year another horrific event occurred: the massacre of the Conestoga Indians on December 27th, 1763. Jacob N. Metzler was eight years old when the Paxtang gang rode into

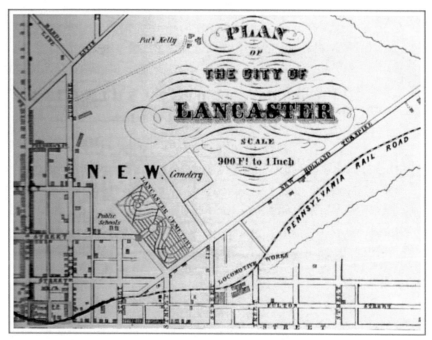

Lancaster City, 1864 Green indicates the graveyard, red the railroad station, and blue the rail line - Courtesy of Linda of Lancaster

Lancaster City and broke into the county jail. They slaughtered 14 Conestoga Indians who were being held in jail under the protection the the county magistrates.

After this horrific event, the bodies were transported east to the Nissley Family Cemetery, nearby Valentine Metzler's farm. The bodies were buried in a common grave in the paupers' section of the cemetery. The cemetery later became the Mennonite Cemetery; still later it was known as the Indian Burial Ground. One can easily imagine Valentine, who was pacifistic in nature, trying to explain this tragedy to his eight year old son Jacob and his other children. But this explains "why John Ruth, in his comprehensive history of Lancaster Mennonites, 'The Earth Is the Lord's,' writes that the Conestogas were buried in Nissley's graveyard on Valentine Metzler's farm."[9]

The Mystery of the Burial Grounds

Both Jacob Nissley and Valentine Metzler were buried in this cemetery, which stood along Cherry Street, between Chestnut and Walnut Streets in Lancaster City. A mound of earth which was removed from the mass grave indicated the spot where the Indians were buried for many years.

In 1833, Indian bones in the cemetery were uncovered by workers laying railroad tracks for the Pennsylvania Railroad. Local historian John Loose believed many of these bones were hauled out along with extra dirt to the railroad embankment. But some of the bones were apparently packed in wooden cases and reburied in the cemetery.[10]

My father, Kenneth Buch Hertzog, worked for most of his life as a foreman for an excavation company called Bilran Excavating, a division of the Horst Group. In the early 1980's, he worked on a housing development called Deer Ford that was built on land that once belonged to Valentine Metzler. He indicated that he had found the grave markers from the Nissley Graveyard. Years laters as he became more involved with his own genealogy research, he went back to the site and discovered that Pennsylvania Power and Electric had put a power line through the area where the grave markers stood, and took no care nor interest in the graveyard. The tombstones were gone or covered up. Perhaps someday I will search the surrounding woods to see if I can find them.

Valentine Becomes a Mennonite Bishop

Throughout the years and all the hardships, it appears that Valentine did not blame God and stood true to his newfound Anabaptist faith. Perhaps these experiences prepared him to face the struggles ahead that the Mennonite church would face in the upcoming years. In the 1760's, Valentine was ordained as a Mennonite Bishop for the district north of Lancaster City.

Boehm's Chapel in 1883

One struggles he faced was dealing with Martin Boehm, who eventually founded Boehm's chapel in 1791. "Boehm was chosen by lot as preacher of the Pequea Mennonite congregation in 1756. His worries over his unworthiness as a minister were dispelled by a powerful conversion experience while plowing his fields in 1758. After this experience he began to preach 'in power' the evangelical message of repentance and salvation by faith. Advanced to the office of bishop in 1759, he continued his preaching, making his famous visit to Virginia in 1761, where he came in contact with the 'Great Awakening' evangelism of George Whitefield and others. On Pentecost 1767, he participated in the 'great meeting' in Mennonite Isaac Long's barn in the Conestoga Valley north of Landis Valley, where he preached to over 1,000 listeners and met Otterbein, who gave Martin Boehm his famous embrace with the words 'Wir sind Brüder!' (We are Brothers). This is considered the founding moment for the establishing of the United Brethren movement."[11]

At first, his fellow Mennonite Bishops welcomed his passionate delivery. But by 1777, their response changed; his style of preaching and evangelization gave the typically reserved and quiet Mennonites pause. Because of this, Martin found himself faced with numerous charges, "including participation with worldly Christians who practiced warfare and oath taking, acceptance of members who were under church discipline, insistence on 'his own particular way,' and failure to accept the community's instruction to confess in his faults."[12] But there was more to it than that. The Great Awakening presented a problem for the Mennonite church because while they certainly embraced the personal conversion experience, the new birth and repentance, they also valued nonconformity, nonresistance, and daily discipleship. Any movement that embraced religious experience as the basis of Christian fellowship was flawed.

Eventually Martin Boehm was excommunicated from the Mennonite church. Valentine Metzler, along with fellow bishops Benjamin Hershey of the Rohrerstown congregation, John Herr I of the Strasburg Congregation, Christian Burkholder of the Groffdale Congregation, Peter Risser of Risser's Congregation, John Lehman of the Mannheim Congregation, Benjamin Landis of Mellinger's Congregation (a great uncle of mine), Christian Hershey of the Habecker Congregation (my great grandfather), Henry Martin from the Weaverland Congregation, and Andrew

Jacob Engle

Hershey and Jacob Brubaker from the Roherstown Congregation, were all signers of Boehm's dismissal. Bohem left to form the United Brethren Church.[13]

In another spiritual upheaval three years later, the Engles of Bainbridge split from the Mennonites of Lancaster to form the Riverside Brethren, which was later renamed the Brethren in Christ. They became known as the River Brethren because they settled along the Susquehanna. Led by Swiss settler Jacob Engle and assisted by his brother John, they promoted a church that practiced the triple immersion in baptism, foot washing, and adherence to plain dress. Bishop Valentine Metzler would have had to help the Mennonite church in Lancaster navigate these tumultuous times.[14]

Bishop Valentine and the Revolution

But the tumult was not just spiritual; it was also political. The Mennonites of Lancaster County were in general wealthy and this made them a special target of the patriots. The Mennonites had gained wealth by living simply, learning how to manage meager land from their time in Germany, and continuing to carry out mutual aid for one another. Because of this and new innovative ways of farming they developed, they became some of the most prosperous and skillful farmers.

This certainly created a spiritual problem among the Mennonites as some Mennonite parents began to focus on helping their children become industrious and wealthy in society's eyes, instead of trying to build eternal riches. One writer even went onto say that prior to the Revolutionary War Mennonites were prone to pride and vanity and would dress in all manners of fashion and fancy clothing.[15]

The government's role in spiritual life divided the Patriots and Bishop Valentine Metzler. The Patriots believed wholeheartedly that God intended government as a positive blessing for mankind. They, like many Protestants, believed that government was ordained by God (Romans 13). To them, this meant a just and equitable human government. So at the start of the Revolutionary War, when the Mennonites refused to join the Patriot cause and not sign up for the local militias, the Patriots considered it heresy and they branded these Anabaptists as enemies of American liberty.

One of the ways that Pennsylvania handled these "non-associators" was through taxation. The initial tax in 1775 was to be equal that of the time spent training the associators; initially this was a tax of 2 Pounds 10 Shillings. Knowing of the Mennonites wealth, the Pennsylvania assembly intended for the peace churches to cover the cost of the war. This tax increased to 3 Pounds 10 Shillings in April of 1776. Then, because so many Pennsylvanians were not signing up to help the associators, the Pennsylvania government increased the non-associator fine to 1 Pound a month. As one can imagine, only those who were truly dedicated pacifists continued to pay the fines; the rest joined up. That same summer, Pennsylvania ordered all non-associators to surrender their rifles. As the Continental Army continued to suffer losses, resentment toward the Mennonites grew. This frustration led to a 20 pound tax in February of 1777. However, this tax was not always collected.[16]

Colonel Bertram Galbraith headed the local militias in Lancaster and continually ran into frustrations at manning the local armies due to the non-associators. At one point, he paraded Mennonites through the streets of Lancaster and locked them up until they either agreed to serve, hired a substitute, or paid the fines.

Some Mennonites did help the war effort and assist ed the Patriots; they just refused to fight. When barracks and a stockade were built in Lancaster in 1776 to house British prisoners, many Mennonites provided lime for it. Bishop Valentine Metzler lent 5 horses to the war effort, as many other Mennonites did, and these were used in hauling ammunition and flour barrels.[17] They also lent wagons as well. In Lancaster specifically, these horses and wagons were used to haul prisoners to the barracks in Elizabeth, New Jersey. Valentine and his associates road along with their wagons and horses to make sure they were returned safely.[18]

This trial of the Mennonite church was not easy for Bishop Valentine Metzler. One can easily imagine the hardship the fines caused members of his congregation, but they supported each other though this difficult time.

The Journey of Valentine's Bible

When Valentine served as Bishop for the Mennonite church, he bought a Froschauer family Bible. This is now a part of the collection at the North Museum at Franklin and Marshall College, Lancaster, PA. In it is written "Valti Metzler, I bought it for 40 shillings, April 27, 1767."[19] Printed in Zurich, Switzerland in 1571, the heavy bound Froschauer volume has brass hinges and clasps, containing marginal references on every page and is pictorial throughout. After his death, the Bible became property of his son Christian. After Christian's death, it was lost until 1832, having either been sold or given away.

The story goes that a tramp, Philip LaMillar, arrived at the house of Christian Hershey near Manheim, PA, carrying a heavy package. When Christian asked what he had in the bag, he replied, "The Holy Scriptures." Upon examining the Bible, Christian determined it was Valentine's Bible and bought it from him for $5.00. He kept it until his death in 1864.

When dividing up his property, neither of Christian Hershey's children, David or Mary, wanted the Bible, for it was too heavy to handle. David put it away in a closet, where it remained until 1871. It was then given to Bishop Jacob Brubacher in whose possession it remained until 1890. Around that time, Christian E. Metzler, a great-grandson of Valentine discovered the Bible's whereabouts. He had been searching for this Bible a long time. Bishop Brubacher gave him the Bible, and it remained with him until 1938. In that year he deposited the Bible for safekeeping

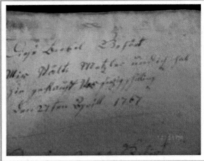

To the left, the outside of the Bible. Above, the inscription inside, written in Valentine's own hand. Below one can see the pictorial depictions of stories contains in each book of the Bible. This Bible can be viewed in the North Museum at Franklin and Marshal College.

with the president of the Lancaster County Historical Society in Lancaster, PA. It was later placed in the North Museum where, as mentioned before, it can still be viewed.[20]

Valentine and Anna had 9 children: 6 sons and 3 daughters. They are as follows:

1. Maria (November 5, 1750 - May 26 1799: Age 49 years) married Bishop Jacob Hostetter the II, who served in the Mannheim district.

2. Abraham (February 24, 1753 - 1818: Age 65 years) married Christina Groff. He took over Valentine's farm.

3. Jacob (May 31, 1755 - March 17 1814: Age 58 years) married to Maria Hess, sister of his sister Anna's husband, Christian Hess.

4. John (November 7, 1757 - 1806: Aged 49 years) married Anna Hess.

5. Anna (January 10, 1760 - December 23, 1816: Aged 56 years) married Christian Hess. He operated Hess's mill and was the leading minister at Hershey's Mennonite Church.

6. Heinrich (June 15, 1762 - November 20, 1837: Aged 75 years) married Mary (Molly) Landis. He was a minster of the Paradise congregation for over 30 years

7. Christian (September 23, 1764 - Aril 11, 1833: Aged 69 years) married Esther Charles.

8. Martin (February 8, 1767 - 1807: Aged 40 years) married Susanna Huber.

9. Elizabeth (October 7, 1769 - February 23, 1795: Aged 26 years) married Jacob Frey, who was a Landisville shoemaker.

Of these children, only Christian and Elizabeth never had any children.

Valentine died on July 24, 1783 at the age of 57, three years before Jacob took over the Peter Meyer farm. Anna Nissley

Metzler died March 29, 1793. They were buried in the graveyard on the former Nissley farm.[21]

How This Connects To The Hertzog Homestead

It is doubtful Valentine ever visited the lands of the Hertzog Homestead, although perhaps his wife Anna may have. His son took over the farm three years after he died. However, Jacob Metzler's life was certainly influenced by his father, influences which carried over to the farm. He learned his coverlet weaving trade that he practiced from his father Valentine and eventually brought Valentine's loom to the plantation. Certainly the struggles of his father and his devout Mennonite upbringing carried with him and influenced his family and conduct. And lastly, without the monies from Valentine's will, he would have never been able to purchase the Hertzog Homestead.

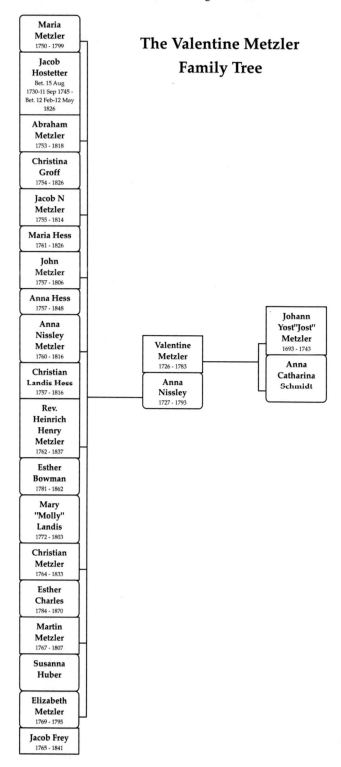

The Valentine Metzler Family Tree

Jacob N. Metzler
and His Plantation

Jacob Metzler: The Coverlet Weaver

Jacob sat, perched on the edge of a wooden bench, and stared past the frame of his barn loom and out the second story window of the forebay over the corn fields. The spring air still crisped his breath as his foot pushed the treadle forward and he used his right hand to push the shuttle behind the threads as he worked on the coverlet. The mid morning sun cast muted shadows over the farm and fell through the double dutch barn doors, warming his back in the coolness of the day. The stream silently trickled below moving past on its way to the Conestoga.

He breathed in deeply, sighed, then looked back at the coverlet before him. When he finished it, it would be added to the collection of coverlets he had for sale in his stone house to the west. His wife Maria would help sell them while he worked the fields and worked the loom. His neighbors might pay in pounds, but an exchange of goods was equally as welcome.

His wife, Maria, was bent over in the garden planting sugar peas that their family would enjoy later in the summer. He had helped her till the earth preparing it for planting. A fence surrounded the rows of future vegetable keeping animals at bay.

The loom continued to whir and clunk as the shuttle shushed back and forth. The faint buzzing of bees lifting from spring flower to spring flower and then to the hives mixed with the sounds of hens and lowing cattle. It was the music of living in the late 1700s. And it helped dull the pain from the loss of his third daughter, who died only six days after she was born.

Jacob Metzler and a Hess Heritage

Jacob Nissley Metzler married Maria Landis Hess on October 15, 1781. She was the daughter of John B. and Susanna Landis Hess, the granddaughter of Jacob and Veronica Bear Hess, and the great-granddaughter of Hans and Magdalane Hess.

The 1778 Stone House Built by Maria's father. Photo courtesy of Jane Metzler Zimmernan.

Maria, along with her brother Christian who married Jacob Metzler's sister, grew up in Lititz, in a log house that her grandfather Jacob Hess had built. The original tract of land actually was requested by Hans Hess, Jacob Hess's father. Hans granted it to Jacob in 1735. The land was heavily wooded and took generations to clear for agricultural use.

The Jacob Hess House built in 1734. The Hess Cemetery lies to the east. Photo courtesy of Jane Metzler Zimmerman.

The Rome Mill that Christian Hess operated. Photo courtesy of Jane Metzler Zimmerman.

In 1778, a stone house was built by Maria's father, but he died during the construction. Christian Hess took over the completion of the house and inherited the farm. He went on to operate the Rome Mill a short distance from the house. In 1795, he passed the house on to his daughter Elizabeth and her husband, Daniel Burkholder, who added a two story addition to the south end in 1800. Daniel was a deacon in the Mennonite Church and his house was one of several that was used for worship prior to the building of the Hess Meeting House in 1856.[1]

Maria Hess: A Descendant of Martyrs

Martyr's Mirror contains graphic accounts of more than 4,000 Christians who endured suffering, torture, and a martyr's death in the 1500 and 1600 in Europe because of their simple faith in the gospel of Christ. Songs, letters, prayers, and confessions appear with the stories of many defenseless Christians who were able to love their enemies and return good for evil. It was written and published in 1659 by a Dutch Mennonite, Thieleman J. van Braght, to strengthen the faith of his fellow believers.

Maria's fourth great grandfather, Hans Jacob Hess, was one such martyr, and his martyrdom is accounted for in this book. Hans was a confirmed minister in the Anabaptist movement in Switzerland. He was arrested for a third time in 1639; his first

An original copy of the Martyr's Mirror

imprisonment occurred in 1637. In both prior events, the Lord had delivered him through the help of fellow prisoners. His first imprisonment last nineteen days; his second lasted eight weeks; and his third last eighty-three weeks. He also at one time was stripped and together with some fellow believers put in iron bonds for 16 weeks.

During these events, his wife was also apprehended, being first imprisoned in the council house, and then in Ottenbach, "where, through bad treatment and unfit food and drink, for sixty-three weeks, she was so impaired in her constitution, and weakened, that she was seized with consumption, and after suffering much misery, died in prison."[2] The property of Hans Hess was seized by the authorities, who realized from the sale of it 4,000 guilders, without restoring anything to the family.

Jacob Metzler Moves on to His Plantation

When John B. Hess, son of the aforementioned Jacob Hess, died in 1783, his 278 acres in Warwick Township were sold to his son John, with the money from the sale being divided up between his wife Susanna and his 10 children, Maria being among them. After Valentine Metzler died in 1783, his wife and 9 children were beneficiaries when his 90 acre farm was sold to Abraham Metzler, his son. This influx of money enabled Jacob to purchase 100 acres from Peter Meyer in Earl Township on April 17th, 1786.[3]

The 1787 Earl Tax records show that he moved onto the farm with two horses and two horned cattle. By the next year, he had three horses and three cows, but returned to having two of each in 1789. This does not change too much fluctuating by one either way until 1811, when he is recorded three horses and six horned cattle. This is consistent with the average for Lancaster County farms which typically had 2.6 horses, 4.5 cattle, and 5 sheep.[4] This was true of the farm when Peter Meyer lived there as well.

Agriculture Transitions

However, things changed in 1811. Actually the change began in 1803 when Jacob's animal inventory increases to 3 horses and 6 horned cattle. A shift was occurring not only for Jacob Metzler, but for the entire Lancaster garden spot as well, a shift from being entirely dependent of crops for revenue to and more diverse crop and livestock system.[5]

One reason for this shift came in the form of a tiny insect, the Hessian Fly, which invaded Lancaster in the 1790s. Though native to Asia, it existed in Europe and arrived to America with the Hessian troops during the American Revolution. This fly devastated farmer's crops, birthing anywhere from two to five generations per year. The female fly could lay anywhere from 250 to 300 eggs on the stem of barley, wheat, and rye. Once the larvae hatched, they fed on the sap and weaken the stem to the plant so that it could not bear grain.

The Hessian Fly

Another potential reason for this shift was an embargo put into place in 1807 by President Thomas Jefferson. He implemented this as a direct result of increased harassment by the British of American ships. This included forcing American men to serve in the British navy and seizures of American goods. Under this embargo, farmers could no longer sell grain overseas. This certainly would cause any farmer to reconsider an over reliance on crops.[6]

The Mysterious Acreage

Besides grains and cattle, inventory records show that Jacob raised grapes and made wine, raised corn, made his own butter, butchered his own animals (having pork, beef, and lard in his inventory list), raised his own potatoes, and made his own soap and bread. Much of this would have been stored in the cellar below the house. Most farmers in the area kept bees as well, though we have no real confirmation that Jacob did so.

In 1792 the farm had 90 acres, suggesting ten were sold off. I have no record of this deed or sale, but it seems that hereafter the farm is pretty consistently shy of 100 acres. In 1793, Jacob Metzler's Plantation (misspelled at Mezel on the tax records) is valued at 599 pounds. This is quite a jump from the assessed value of 250 pounds in 1789. It jumped in value again in 1797 to 950 pounds and then again in 1805 to 2000 pounds. This shift in valuation was the result of a shift toward an American system of government, a stabilization in the economy, and an increase in the number of people in Jacob's household.

Coverlet Weaving as a Supplemental Business

As previously mentioned, Jacob N. Metzler worked as a weaver, a business he learned from his father. Jacob is last recorded as a weaver in a 1801 tax record. This was prior to the quilt era which began in the mid-1800s; he wove coverlets. This meant that he had a loom (most likely his father's), a spinning wheel and reel, a wool wheel, and a cotton wheel; all things were found in widow Maria Metzler's inventory list at her death. It seems doubtful that he would have worked loom in his 15 by 30 foot house, especially with 6 children in the house. It seems more likely that he ran the loom out of his barn.

Coverlet weaving was a sensible supplemental business for a farmer. As can be seen later, the farm had sheep and raised flax, providing some of the necessary material for coverlet weaving. There are other items of a weaving nature in Maria Metzler's inventory list: 70 yards of linen cloth, 18 yards of low linen, 16 table clothes, and flax and yarn.

This is an example of a barn loom, the type that Jacob Metzler would have had.

While some coverlets are owned by descendants of the Jacob Metzler family, there is no evidence they were made by Jacob Metzler. Most coverlets from that time period were not signed or dated. While the loom operation most likely took place in the barn, the sales of his wares took place out of the house.

It is interesting that Maria Metzler kept the loom for 12 years after his death. With the materials she had on hand, she was probably weaving as well.

The Indian Door

An Indian door exists in the house and was potentially used as a part of his weaving endeavors. According to William Blair, a Historic Lancaster Walking Tour guide, such doors served to keep the inhabitants of a home safe if it were attacked by Indians. The door on the Jacob Metzler Planation is built so that a bottom wood panel can slide up covering the glass in case of an Indian attack, thus protecting the home. It is doubtful it was ever installed with such a purpose in mind.

In conversations I had with the Lancaster Historical Society, they believed, due to him being a weaver, that he most likely used the door to indicate when he was open for business. When the panel was down, he was open; when the panel was up, he was closed. This does make sense.

The Indian Door that Jacob Metzler may have used to conduct his coverlet weaving business. Photo by Sierra Thomas.

But Clarke Hess, a descendant of the aforementioned Hess family and an expert on Lancaster architecture and antiques, disagrees with this assessment. First off, by the 1760's Indian attacks has ceased to exist. He dates the earliest appearance of such doors to the early 1800's. This implies that Peter Meyer or Jacob Metzler may not have installed this door at all. Rather Jacob H. Metzler added the door to the dwelling when he expanded the house and added the second story. Instead of being used to protect against Indian attacks or to sell coverlets out of the home, the door had a more common function. It acted like a door shutter, protecting against storms yet allowing ventilation.[7]

Water from the Well

A forty foot hand dug well lined with limestone supplied the plantation with water. This may have been dug by Peter or possibly by Jacob. With a dedicated water source running through the property, digging a well may not have been a priority for them. Initially the water was accessed via a bucket and then later a pump. The original pump still exists in a photograph from 1950. The well still exists today, and still has potable water.

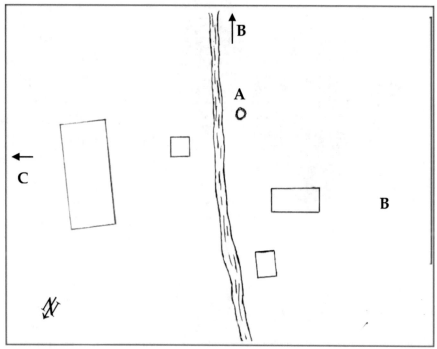

A. *The forty foot, limestone lined, hand dug well that Peter Meyer or Jacob Metzler built.*
B. *The potential placement of the orchards* C. *The Metzler Family Cemetery*

The Beginnings of Metzler's Mennonite Cemetery

When Jacob and Maria moved onto the farm, they brought with them a daughter, Maria (Mary), who was born December 29, 1787. Susanna, their second daughter, was born on August 14, 1788 and lived to be 18 years old. Their third daughter lived only six days. Anna was born on May 18, 1790 and died May 24, 1790. She was the first person buried in the Metzler Family Cemetery, located about 100 yards to the east behind the barn. The grief must have been great for he intentionally placed the graveyard behind the barn so it could not been seen from the house. This cemetery later became the Metzler's Mennonite Church Cemetery. Anna's grave marker, along with those of the rest of the Jacob Metzler Family, can still be seen in this cemetery today. The fourth daughter of Jacob and Maria was also named Anna. She was born on December 7, 1791 and lived one year, four months, and eleven days.

The birth of Elizabeth on September 5, 1794 gave a fifth daughter to the Metzler family. She later married Peter Kilhafer and lived to be 74. A third Anna was born on April 7, 1796 and lived longer than the other Annas. She married Henry B. Eberly and lived to be 42 years of age. They moved to Orrville, Ohio. Jacob's seventh daughter was born on February 6, 1800. Her name was Barbara. She married Daniel Myers and lived 63 years. The family's final daughter, Veronica, was born March 5, 1802. She married David Brubaker and lived to be 39 years old.

Jacob N. Metzler had one son, Jacob Hess Metzler, born May 17, 1798. Being his only male heir, the farm was destined to be given to him, but not until he was twenty-one years of age.[8]

The Death of Jacob Metzler

Jacob N. Metzler wrote in his will that "Maria shall have the right of all the income of my plantation until my son Jacob shall arrive to the age twenty-one years and all my children shall remain with her and assist her to do her work as in my life time." He charged her to send the children to school, pay the yearly tax, and keep his plantation in good repair, especially the fences and timbers. These fences were particularly important as they kept cattle and wildlife out of his gardens and fields.

In the will, he authorized the sale of 25 acres of the farm should the executors of his will deem it necessary. His only qualification was that it be acreage that would do least damage to his other land. The monies from the sale were to be distributed for the building of a house, barn, or stable.

Jacob Nissley Metzler died at fifty-five years of age on March 17th, in 1814. His son was 15 years old. This meant that for the next six years, Jacob, Maria, Barbara, Veronica, and the other siblings helped their mother take care of the plantation. Technically, the farm remained the property of Jacob N. Metzler

Left: *Cover of the Jacob N. Metzler Bible.* **Below Left:** *Jacob N. Metzler's signature.* **Below Right:** *A list of births and significant dates for the Jacob N. Metzler Family. He bought this Bible for 1 pound, 13 shillings and 9 Pence on April 2, 1782.* **Bottom:** *Jacob writes "This Bible belongs to me, Jacob Metzler, written on 12 of August 1798." It is not know why he felt the need to write this 16 years after he purchased the Holy Book.*

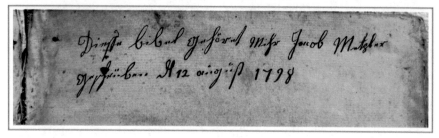

until his son's twenty-first birthday. The April 1st, 1815 District tax records record him as still owning the farm of ninety acres with a stone and wood house fifteen by thirty feet and a stone barn 65 by 30 feet worth about $6300 dollars.

The Inventory List and Jacob's Bible

Maria followed him in death 12 years later. Maria Metzler's Inventory list, compiled at her death, sheds a little more light on what life was like. I have included the list at the end of this section. The family apparently was educated, and perhaps wealthy enough, to own 16 books, perhaps an extravagance for people trying to eek out a farming existence. There was a grandfather clock in the house, bellows to stoke the fire, a German bible (now owned by Jane Metzler Zimmerman), and a sleigh. And they drank coffee.

One note on the Jacob N. Metzler German Bible. Writing on the inside cover the the back of the Bible indicates that he bought the Bible for 1 pound, 13 shillings and 9 Pence on April 2, 1782. He indicates the Bible as belonging to him by writing "This Bible belongs to me, Jacob Metzler, written on 12 of August 1798." The Bible itself was published in Germantown in 1776, the year American earned its independence. It records family birth, marriage, and death records on the back pages. [9]

How This Connects To The Hertzog Homestead

The Hertzog Homestead was known as the Jacob Metzler Plantation during this time. As far as we can ascertain, he did not change or add any structures to the property. His daughter became the first person to be buried in the Metzler Cemetery, originally Jacob Metzler's family cemetery. He continued clearing the land for farming. Last of all, West Metzler Road, East Metzler Road, Metzler's Mennonite Church (Meetinghouse), and Metzler's One Room Schoolhouse were all named after him.

The Jacob Metzler Family Tree

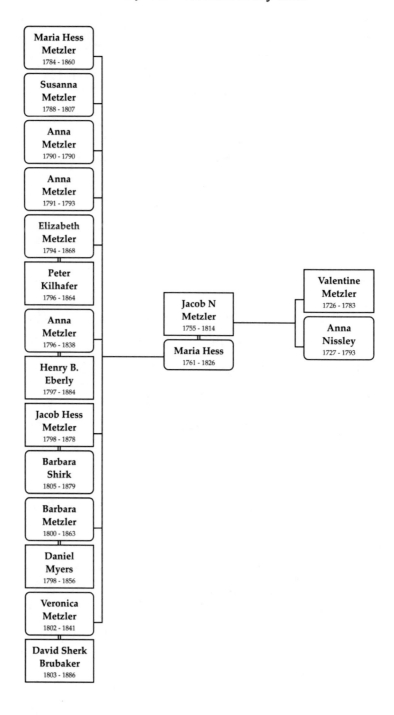

Above: Fractal of a Farewell Bird for Maria Metzler done in 1836, 10 years after her death. Below: Fractal of a Farewell Bird for Jacob Metzler done in 1837, 23 years after his death.

Maria Metzler's Inventory List

...tels, Rights and Credits, which were of Mary
Metzler late of Earl township, Lancaster County
in the State of Pennsylvania, Widow, deceased
at the time of her death, to wit.

	Doll.	cts
Cash	133	09
Bond from Henry Stoner with the Interest to 5th June 1826	257	15
Note from Henry Stoner with interest to 5th June 1826	150	17
Note from Christian Metzler with interest to 5th June 1826	269	54
Book accounts	45	57
Clock and case bequeathed to her daughter Mary ——— 15.00		
Goods bequeathed to her Son Jacob, to wit:		
1 Stove ——— 1..50		
1 German bible ——— 5..00		
1 steelyard ——— 0..80	22	30
1 Stove and pipe	10	00
1 Clothes case	4	00
Linen cloth about 70 yards	28	00
Tow linen about 18 yards	3	60
16 Table cloths	4	80

Item	Dol.	cts.
A lot of old cloths	2	00
1 bedstead	0	40
Beddings and 1 bedstead	24	30
2 Chests	1	50
Wearing apparel	8	00
6 boxes	1	00
10 books	3	00
5 Chairs	1	25
3 Tables	1	25
1 spinning wheel and 1 reel	0	50
Tin and pewter ware	7	50
Earthen ware	5	00
Kitchen dresser	0	75
3 Iron pots, 2 pans, 1 kettle	3	50
1 Copper kettle		00
1 wool wheel, 1 cotton wheel	1	75
Side saddle	0	12½
2 small kettles	1	00
2 tubs, and 2 buckets	0	50
1 tub and a stand	1	50
Pork and beef	2	50
Bag with corn	0	00
2 barrels	0	50
3 buckets, 1 Cann	0	75
Keg with wine	2	00
4 small tubs	1	00
1 Churn, and 2 barrels	0	75
Potatoes	0	25
Lard	1	00
Butter and tallow	0	80

	Dolls	cts
Soap	0	50
Flax and yarn	1	50
Salt about 1 bus	0	75
1 loom and small basket	0	40
2 looking glasses 1 shears	0	30
6 bags 1 keg	1	75
1 Dough trough and bread baskets	0	40
Wash line & brush	0	40
Basket & sundries	0	18
Trough & 2 bags	0	25
1 Hog	1	50
1 Cow	10	00
1 Sleigh	1	00
Bed cord	0	35
Pot hook fire shovel and tongs	1	25
Bellows	0	37½
Coffee kettle &c	0	12½
	1028	92½

Taken and appraised by us the sub
scribers, the 5th day of June A.D. 1826.

Henry Stoner

Jacob Noll

Exhibited into the Registers office of Lancaster the 6th day
of June Anno Domini 1826 in Testimon Mejor junr
and by and under the
Appraisers & testes afores
Cram John Bachman junr
Deputy Reg

By Jacob Metzler

Jacob H. Metzler:
An Era of Expansion
and Growth

K. Scott Hertzog

A New House, A New Church

Jacob H. Metzler sat on a chair watching twilight settle over the two story house he and his hired help were building. An occasional bat darted over the darkening sky and the day birds were quieting. At the other end of the log house, he could hear Catherine cooing in Barbara's arms. He smiled. Jacob leaned back in the chair and reflected.

That past year had wrought so much change. Maria, his mother who had lived in this house, had passed away last year. Remembering how cramped the little one story house he and his seven siblings had grown up in, he and Barbara had decided to add a second story and extend the footprint of the house southward. They both hoped for a large family. The plans had actually been developing before his mother had passed. He took a deep breath in then sighed. He missed her.

Yesterday, the Society of Mennonites had broken ground to build the new Mennonite Church 100 yards to the east from where he was sitting now. He and his wife had donated the land to the society of Mennonites along with the family cemetery where his father and mother were buried. Some of his siblings were buried there as well. His only caveat was that the church be named after his family. God had been good to them.

The Slow Transition

On February 9, 1824, Jacob N. Metzler's widow Maria and his brother Christian Metzler officially handed over the reigns of the farm to Jacob H. Metzler. Jacob H. Metzler was 25 years old. He was deeded 70 acres of the 95 acre farm. The 70 acres were valued at 1801 pounds, 5 shillings, and five pence.

There is discrepancy between what 1820s tax records show as a 90 acre farm and what the deed describes as a 95 acre farm. This does not seem uncommon for that time. Actual recorded acreage often wavered a little bit.

Though Jacob H. Metzler was officially deeded the farm in 1824, Earl Tax Records indicate him as owning the 70 acre farm as early as 1820 with his mother owning the other 25 acres of the farm, presumably the lot surrounding the log house. The most likely interpretation of this discrepancy in dates is that the deed was officially filed four years later after it was created. This, too, was not uncommon. Together they own 3 horses and 5 horned cattle.

According to oral tradition, Maria moved into the log home on these twenty-five acres. Some have speculated that a log home was built for Maria Metzler, across the road from the stone house in what is now Reuben Oberholtzer's garden. There is little concrete proof of this. Some suggest that Jacob N. Metzler's Will that the executors of said Will would build her a "Clevor Widow Seat". I had a difficult time determining exactly what this means, but one possible interpretation of this is the log house. However, further research suggests that this log house was probably the original house on the farm, built long before Maria Metzler retired there.

As part of the purchase of the farm, Jacob H. Metzler paid Maria Metzler, his mother, 650 pounds due April 1st of each year for the duration of her life. This would turn out to be only two more years from dating of the deed, six years from when he officially took over the farm. He paid this in cash or through any of the following items equal in value: twelve bushels of wheat, twelve bushels of rye and corn, twelve bushels of oats, five bushels of potatoes, 8 pounds of heckled flax, four pounds of wool, fifty pounds of beef, one cow fed in winter with good hay and pasture in summer, a piece of the garden, one bushel of dry apples, and if there was fruit, a half barrel of cyder (sic), six pots of apple butter and apples as many as she should choose, and a right to raise twelve fowl. Clearly, the widow of Jacob N. Metzler was very well provided for. This also gives us a pretty clear picture about what was being raised and grown on the farm.

Maria Metzler died on May 10, 1826. She was 65 years old. She was laid to rest beside her husband and children who died before her in the Metzler Family cemetery.

The Ghost of Maria Metzler

It was an early April morning in 1986 when Douglas Hertzog, my brother, woke up and began to get ready for work. He worked part time as a laborer for our father, Kenneth Buch Hertzog, a foreman for Bilran excavating, a division of Horst Group. As he was pulling on his jeans, he glanced out the window of our bedroom on the second floor of the Jacob Metzler Plantation and froze. At 4:30 AM, he saw an old woman, stooped over with a shawl around her head, reaching down and working in the garden, near where the log house once stood.

Thinking it had to be his imagination, he shook his head and went to the bathroom to brush his teeth. My brother has always been a rationale and more logical oriented guy. When he went back and looked out the window she was still there, hunched over and working the garden at this ungodly hour. Later, when he looked out, she was gone.

While some may argue that there were many women who had lived in that log house over the years and that it could have been any of them, Maria Metzler was the only one to have died there. Peter Meyer's wife passed after he moved to York County, PA. In subsequent generations, all other women would have passed away in the main house. So it is my belief that who he saw was the ghost of Maria Metzler. To my knowledge, no one else has ever seen this apparition.[1]

The Plantation House: Upward and Outward

The house contains no date stone, but according to a Pennsylvania Historic Survey prepared by John J. Synder, the two-story dwelling was most likely built between 1820 to 1845. He based this conclusion on generalized stylistic evidence and comparisons with other local houses bearing date stones. This fits with my assessment of the house as well.

Tax records until 1815 indicate the house was one story. Until 1820, the Maria Metzler and her children were running the farm, and it seems unlikely that they would have started such a big building project during this time. Considering the money Jacob H. Metzler is paying to Maria during the 1820's, it also seems unlikely that he expand ed the house, or the barn for that matter, immediately after taking over the farm. The expansions to both buildings probably did not take place until the 1830's, after he had established himself on the farm and no longer had to support his mother.

One of the stone quarries off of High Road.

The Farm Quarries

Evidence suggests that Jacob H. built the house himself, most likely with hired help or the help of neighbors. Neighbors often helped each other build and harvest as was needed. Sale bills after his retirement and death show that he had the quarrying tools and logging equipment, enabling him modify the one story structure. The farm had at least two places stone was quarried. The one quarry, pictured below, is clearly visible from High Road that runs along side the current farm. The reality was and still is that the soil on this farm, while extremely good and productive, is also very rocky. He most likely pulled stones from the fields as well.

The Plantation Lime Kiln

For a long time, I did not know there was a lime kiln on the farm. It makes sense that if Jacob H. Metzler quarried his own rock, he also made his own lime for mortar, white-washing, and various other uses for lime. This was most likely the same kiln Peter Meyer built and used.

I was giving a tour of the property at the 275th Metzler Reunion, when David Horning, who had worked on the farm during the 1950s, asked if there was a lime kiln on the place. This was the first time I had ever heard about it. He had vague recollections of its existence, and thought that it

The place originally thought to be where the lime kiln once existed.

might be out at the hill, pictured on the left. I later asked Richard Buch, who also worked on the farm, if he knew about the farm having a lime kiln. He asked if it was out at the hill. He, too, however seemed uncertain as to whether that was the actual location or not. As a side note, both these men are descendants of Jacob N. Metzler.

This took me to the 1875 Atlas, which, according to Dr. Ken Miller, an authority on lime kilns in Lancaster County, PA, marked most of the lime kilns. However, the Jacob Metzler Plantation lime kiln was not marked on the map.

I spent an evening walking through the farm with Sam Oberholtzer, a laborer who worked on the farm in the later 1950s and early 1960s. When I asked him about the lime kiln, he thought he knew exactly where it was. It was on the hill where Richard and David thought it was. But after searching the hill thoroughly, we found little evidence of any kiln.

On a Saturday in late July 2013, the Oberholtzer brothers and sisters had a family gathering. Many of them had worked on the farm when the great, great grandchildren of Jacob H. Metzler owned it. I had the privilege of sitting with them for an hour, hearing them tell stories regarding what it was like working on the farm. Eventually I turned the discussion to the lime kiln. Sam's bothers disagreed with him as to the location, stating that it existed just beyond where the tobacco shed had stood, where the land came to a point. They were right.

The aforementioned Ken Miller, a retired professor at Millersville University, visited the farm at my request soon after this meeting. When he investigated the area the Oberholtzer brothers had indicated, he pointed out to me the burned sandstone that would have lined the inner walls of the kiln.

Jacob would have made his lime by burning limestone in this kiln. The kiln, located beside a road, gave him easy access to dump stone into the kiln. It had an egg-cup shaped burning chamber surrounded by sandstone inner walls. The exterior walls toward the south were limestone. There was an eye or inlet for air at the base. To make lime, limestone was crushed into 1.5 - 2.5 inch rocks, which allowed for breathing during the firing. Dome

Above: The location of the lime kiln on the property, the collapsed stone from the kiln is visible in the picture. Left: The current condition of the lime kiln. Below: A portion of the inner chamber sandstone wall scarred by limestone burning.

shaped layers of alternating limestone and wood would be built up over the eye. When the kiln was fully loaded, the kindling was lit at the bottom and fire slowly spread up through the layers. Once all layers were burnt through, the lime was cooled and raked out. Typically it would take around a week to make lime. It would take Jacob and his family a day to load, three days to fire, two days to cool, and a day to unload.[2]

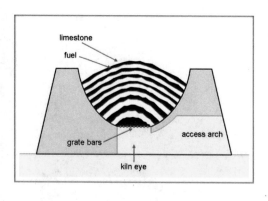

Lime was important, helping lower the acidity of fields, helping to produce and grow better hay, acted as a disinfectant for privies, and for Jacob H. Metzler, it was a key ingredient in mortar, plaster, and white wash.

Inside the Two Story House

When Jacob H. Metzler began building the walls of the house, he did not entirely destroy the one story dwelling. He used most of the 30 foot northern wall and the 15 foot wall to the west side of the house along the bank and incorporated them into the two story stone structure. As said before, the northwest corner of the house has sandstone only coming down to the top of the first floor. This seems to confirm that he used part of the original wall.

The sandstone corners are an interesting feature of the house. Since sandstone is not native to the farm, it was most likely imported from the Bowmansville, PA or Brickerville, PA areas, both of which are known for sandstone. Brickerville has entire houses built of sandstone.

Why the sand stone corners? Some people claim that sandstones' resilience over time helped shore up the house; however, limestone has a similar durability. Jacob H. seems to be flexing some artistic muscle here. There are only a few other houses that have sandstone corners like those crafted by Jacob H. Metzler.

Jacob H. Metzler built the two story house using a federalist style with four bay facade that included windows that

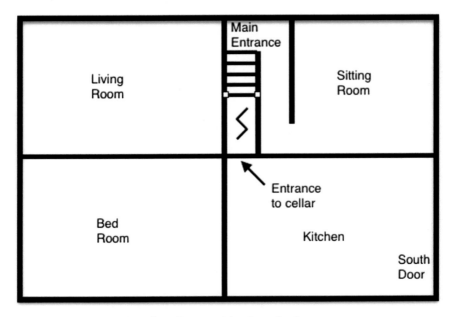

First floor diagram of the plantation house

had a six over six sash. The two foot thick stone walls were actually not solid stone, but rather two layers of stone with crushed stone in between. This allowed for water that seeped in from the outside to drain down. It also functioned as kind of a natural insulation.

The first floor of the house had four rooms. The kitchen, as referenced through oral tradition, was always in the southwestern corner room with an entrance facing the south. It also had a doorway that led to the cellar, though

The built-in corner cupboard complete with rat-tail hinges and a keystone. Photo by Sierra Thomas.

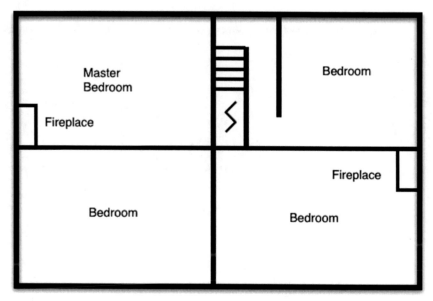

Second floor diagram of the plantation house

there was a southern outside entrance to the cellar as well.

The main entrance to the house was on the eastern side toward the barn, fronted by the Indian door. The door opened up into a hallway that led to the kitchen with a door along the hallway that opened into a smaller room, a sitting room, on the left. To the right, a door opened into a living room complete with the built-in corner cupboard and the German Bible Closet. There was an open staircase to the right of the hallway leading up to the second floor.

The upstairs also had four rooms. The stairs up lead onto an upper hallway that turned left around a banister. This led back to what seems to have been the master bed room with a built in fireplace. A stove pipe came up through the floor of this room, as it did with all the upstairs floor at one point in the house's history. The southwest room above the kitchen also had a built in fireplace, though not as fancy. Above the stairs from the first to the second floor were stairs leading from the second floor to the attic. The attic has a cedar smoke room, pictured on the prior page, near the northern chimney.

Cedar Smoke Room

Other than the Bible closet, there was only one other closet in the house, and that seems to have been newer, perhaps constructed, during Jacob S. Metzler's time or during Daniel Buch's residence. It was on the first floor and was torn down when a bathroom was installed for the bed and breakfast. It was the only real closet in the original house. With the exception of this closet, clothes were hung on pegs. They did not have near the amount of clothing we have today.

The Barn Expansion

The barn was extended in this time period as well. Typical of many farms during that time period, Jacob H. Metzler added a wagon drive through beyond the southern gable of the barn, thus adding one bay.[3] He tore down the southern stone gable to the top of the first floor; the area above the drive through extended his tobacco growing space. The new southern wall of the barn contained a corncrib, giving him additional space for corn storage. The wagon drive through would also have allowed him to store machinery as well.

Jacob H. Metzler's Family

On May 24th, 1825, Jacob H. Metzler married Barbara, daughter of John and Catherine Shirk. He was 27 years old and she was 20. The next year she gave birth to their first daughter named Catherine, in honor of her grandmother; two years later twins boys were born and named in honor of both grandfathers. Samuel and Barbara were born afterwards and completed the family.

Their first daughter, Catherine Shirk Metzler, was born on August 4, 1826. She later married her second cousin's first born son, Samuel H. Hess. Her sister, Barbara Shirk Metzler, was born April 29, 1837, and married Joseph R. Rupp, born on May 11, 1834. They lived on the farm at Diamond Springs that later contained the two trolley stations; these are later discussed. Joseph R. Rupp died on January 11, 1896, and Barbara died on April 16th, 1904, at four O'clock on a Saturday afternoon, due to complications with pneumonia.[4] Joseph R. Rupp was a second cousin to the Joseph W. Rupp who rebuilt what became known as Rupp's mill discussed earlier in this book.

The older of the twins, John S. Metzler, was born on October 10, 1828. He was older than Jacob S. Metzler by one and half hours. He married Mary Ann Burkholder on January 15, 1852. Having several children by time the Civil War broke out, he was exempt from war duties. However, his brother Jacob Shirk Metzler was not. Jacob married Mary Ann Landis on December 8, 1957. He registered as a conscientious objector during the Civil War. Jacob eventually would become the third Jacob Metzler to live on the Jacob Metzler Plantation.

Jacob H. Metzler's youngest child was Samuel Shirk Metzler, born July 7, 1832. In 1855 he married Rebecca E. Yundt, and they moved to Chicago the same year. He was called a veterinary surgeon in the census of 1880. Contrary to his twin brothers

An undated photo of Samuel S. Metzler

noninvolvement stance during the Civil War, he served as a private in Company "H" in the 17th Illinois Calvary during the war between the States. His date of muster was January 22, 1864.[5]

Company H served with the Second Battalion commanded by Major Matlack, and they occupied the port of Glasgow, Illinois. The entire detachment was kept busy dealing with guerrilla bands of rebel sympathizers who hassled the local inhabitant and disrupted telegraph lines. They managed to keep the rebels in check.

"The reported presence of the rebel Colonel Thornton, with 1,500 men, induced an order from General Rosecrans, through General Fisk, for a movement from Glasgow, northward and westward, in search of Thornton. Pursuant thereto, Major Matlack moved, with all his mounted force and a squadron of the Ninth Cavalry, Missouri State Militia, to Chillicothe, on the Hannibal and St. Joseph Railroad. Here, reinforced by 500 militia, the column was divided into three detachments, and thoroughly scoured the whole country, from the railroad, southward and westward, to the river. No enemy was found, but the presence of the troops reassured the Union men of that country, and held their enemies in check."[6]

Growing up on the Metzler Plantation gave him the skills needs to work with his horses in the calvary. Potentially, he learn some of his veterinarian skills while in the service. He was discharged on February 13, 1865.[7]

The Beginnings of Metzler's Mennonite Church

In 1827, Jacob H. Metzler sold 60 perches to the Society of Mennonites (now Metzler's Mennonite Church) for a Meeting House and cemetery. The land for the cemetery included the Metzler family graveyard. The deed stated that if the property ever ceased to be a Mennonite church, the property would revert back to the heir's of Jacob Metzler. As said in the deed: "A deed of conveyance, dated the 26th of May one thousand eight hundred

Metzler's Mennonite Church in the early 1900s.

and twenty-seven... for the use of said society...that if at any time, the said premises shall not be used or occupied by the said Mennonite Society, as and for their uses and purposes, as remained and declared so forth, with the intention or perpetual abandonment of the same, in that case, the hereby granted premises shall descend and revert back to the said Jacob Metzler, his heirs, and assigns of the adjoining of the adjoining premises." The deed also stated that only Mennonites could serve as trustees in the church and that non-Mennonites could not preach, though they could be buried in the graveyard. Jacob H. Metzler later would sell an additional 85 perches to Metzler's Mennonite Church in 1864.

The original frame and log meeting house was twenty-eight by thirty-four feet, and typified the Mennonite meeting houses of the time. Receiving donations from $2.00 to $40.00, the building cost a total of $420.24. Fifty-five people contributed to the building fund. It is possible this indicates the size, or at least the number of working men, who were in the congregation when it started.[8]

The Evolution of the Plantation

The 1824 deed between Maria Metzler and Christian Metzler indicates that the original 25 acres given to Maria for her widow's house was to come under the ownership of Jacob H. Metzler when Maria died. When this happened, this brought the farm back to 95 acres.

In 1845, he purchased 24 acres and 50 perches from Samuel Brown and 18 acres and 146 perches from Henry Brown. He allegedly bought these tracts of land to make equal farms for his twin sons, John S. Metzler and Jacob S. Metzler. This brought his acreage up to around 138 acres. The additional farm acreage is reflected in 1850 tax records, which record him as owning 133

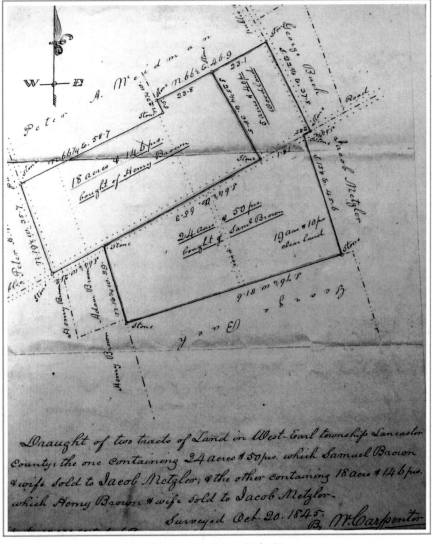

A sketch of the land Jacob bought for his sons.

127

acres of improved land and 20 acres of unimproved land valued at $15,000.00.[9]

A Successful Farmer

By 1850 Jacob H. Metzler ran a very successful farm. In 1820, he had owned 70 acres; now he owned 133 tillable acres, with unimproved acreage increasing the number to 153 acres. The plantation contained the most acreage at this point. The two horses and two horned cattle that Jacob had when he took over the farm grew to nine horses, five milch cows, twelve head of cattle, eight sheep, and eleven swine, valued at $600. He owned $400 dollars in farm machinery. The farm had brought in 400 bushels of wheat, 600 bushels of Indian corn, 500 bushels of oats, 40 bushels of Irish potatoes, $10 dollars in orchard produce, 600 pounds of butter, and 25 tons of hay.[10] This gives us a good picture of what was being raised on the farm and how the farm was being utilized. Needless to say, the Sweitzer barn was chocked full with crops.

This is another reason John J. Snyder's earlier estimate as to when the two story house was built makes sense. With his prosperity and his ability to purchase neighboring land, he seems to be financially able to build the two story farmhouse.

By 1850, his daughter Catherine had married. The September 11, 1850 Census shows there were six people living at the plantation. Jacob H. was 52 years old (though the census has him marked as 50) with his occupation marked as a farmer, his wife Barbara was 45, John S. is 21 and marked as a farmer, Jacob S., also 21, is marked as a laborer, Samuel S. is marked also as a laborer, and Barbara S. is 13.[11]

1860 was a year of transition for the family. Although the deed is not recorded until 1865, it appears that by 1860 the main farm had switched hands. Jacob H. Metzler now owned 1 acre of improved land and 18 acres of unimproved land. He owned two cows and three swine valued at $90 dollars; 10 bushel of Irish

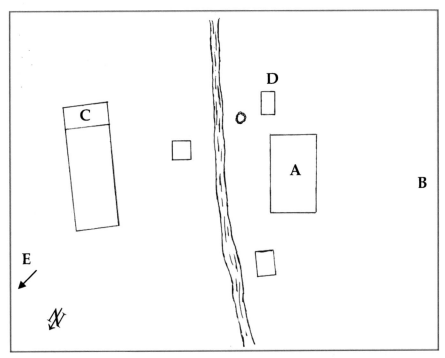

A. The expanded two-story plantation house B. The lime-kiln C. The lengthen Swietzer barn with machinery drive through D. The butcher house E. Metzler's Mennonite Church

Potatoes; orchard products at a $5 dollar value; 150 pounds of butter; and slaughtered animals valued at $36 dollars.[12] The last item is the first time we see mentioned a quantitative amount of slaughtering.

The Slaughterhouse

There is a block house on the property that we always grew up referring to as the "Butcher House". We only ever butchered chickens there one time; it was during the Avian Flu in the early 1980s. Mostly, my parents used it as a garden shed; today it is used as the offices for the Hertzog Homestead Bed and Breakfast and the Spa Cottage. This block house was built in 1945 by Elmer Metzler Buch; his initials are written into the floor along with the date.

Is this butcher house on the original site on which Jacob H. Metzler butchered animals, or did he butcher at a completely different location on the farm? According to hired hands that worked the farm in the 1950's and 1960's, this block building was never used for butchering. It functioned as a wash room and coal bin, an interesting combination. So why did my family grow up calling this a butcher house when no butchering ever took place in it? There is no clear answer, but when I asked my grandmother this, she just chuckled and said that hired hands were much younger than she was. She remembered animals being butchered on this location.

The 1858 Sale and What It Tells Us

Jacob H. Metzler passed the farm off to his son Jacob in 1858. On February 23, 1858, he held a public sale. He had obviously decided to retire. The items sold tell us much about what the farm must have been like in the 1850s. At the sale, he sold:

three milch cows	other cattle
1 sow	4 shoats (newly weaned, young pigs)
8 pigs	a threshing machine and horse power
1 plantation wagon	a corn sheller
a cart	hay and wood ladders
a revolving rake	spike and shovel harrows
ploughs	single, double, and Treble Trees
horse gears	log, cow, and halter chains
dung hook	jack screw (similar to a modern jack)
forks and rakes	quarrying tools
chestnut rails	oats by the bag

tables	beds and a bedstead
chairs	1 cooking stove
chests	1 ten plate stove and pipe
copper kettle	pots and pans
Iron Kettles	apple Butter by the crock
potatoes by the bushel	a log for stave wood (used for making barrels)

And by the way, do not bring liquor. One has to wonder he added this statement. From this list, we get an idea of how the house was furnished. It seems clear he was downsizing his own operation.

That he had a threshing machine is telling. These machines were expensive and in many cases farmers would band together to get one, but Jacob H. owned one outright. In the farming boom of the 1820s, hand threshing, as it was traditionally done on the threshing floors of his forebay barn, was exchanged in favor of a machine. Threshing was moved from the barn to the fields.[13] That he had a

The 1858 Public Sale Bill

machine for threshing meant he was raising a lot of grain, so it makes sense that he had bags of oats at the sale. And as a side

131

note, that he had a corn sheller seems to indicate he was raising corn as well, a fact verified in tax records.

Jacob H. also had a fairly big orchard. He was selling apple butter by the crock. Later sales records indicate that the Metzlers were making vinegar and selling cider as well. Having a log for staves enabled them to make barrels for such liquids.

Where Did Jacob Metzler Go?

After the sale, Jacob H. Metzler is listed in records as owning 1 acre of improved land. One of the discussions I had with my cousin Jane Metzler Zimmerman regarded what sort of home was on this one acre of improved land that he and Barbara moved into, if there was a house on this acreage at all, and if he and Barbara even moved. We know the 16 by 13 foot summer house, the original log house, existed. Was this house on this acreage?

Jacob H. Metzler's "Declaration of Rights" gives some indication of what happened. It has a section which reads as follows:

> (The) granted premises (the 77 acres), to and
> for the use of the said Jacob Metzler and
> Barbara his wife, during their joint
> lives and the   lifetimes of the survivor of them,
> the use and possession and occupation of the
> dwelling house, stable and other
> improvements, and lot of one acre of
> land (as now   fenced off and occupied by
> them)

What is meant by the "occupation of the dwelling house"? How do we interpret the "lot of one acre of land (as now fenced off and occupied by them)"?

Perhaps they moved into the 16 by 13 log summer house, and the one acre of improved land and the 18 acres of unimproved land were attached to this property. Indeed, the more I read the above statement and consider the position of and the qualification

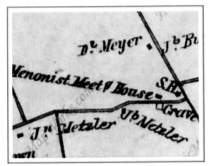 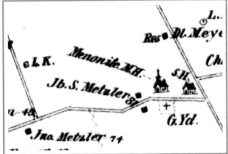

The 1864 and 1875 Atlas Maps

of the word "land", this seems to be a plausible interpretation of Jacob H. Metzler's intent, if not the correct one. In fact, it would make sense since Maria Metzler, his mother, would have lived there when he took over the farm in 1820.

There is one complication though. In 1860, when tax records show Jacob H. Metzler as having the 1 acre of improved land, he is living with his wife, Barbara, his daughter, Barbara, and a woman named Mary. That is four people that moved into the log house that was potentially last lived in by Maria Metzler. By the 1860s, how normal would this have been? How comfortable would the 16 by 13 house have been? Peter Meyer would have originally had to start a family in it, so it was possible. Another point is that Jacob also had 2 milk cows and 3 swine. These animals are not on the one acre since there was no stable or barn on it.

Another theory, and the one to which I currently ascribe, is that when the "Declaration of Rights" mentions that Jacob and Barbara have "the use and possession and occupation of the dwelling house, stable and other improvements," this means that, despite the house being deeded to his son, he retained the right to use the limestone plantation house and the stable for his animals. The occupied one acre gave him a place to garden.

The main plantation house would have certainly been a full house. Along with his four member household, Jacob S. Metzler and his newly married wife, Mary Ann, would have been living there, along with Harrison Fronkhouser, 46, (a farm laborer), Ann Eliza Landis, 19, (a sister to Mary Ann), Augustus Hoy, 32 (laborer), and Francis Hoy (26) (laborer). That means nine people were living in the main dwelling house. In this scenario, the farm laborers most likely lived in the log house.

1850's Hand Corn Sheller

So Jacob H. Metzler and his wife were legally guaranteeing the right to continue living in the 2 story stone house; they could continue to use the dwelling house, the stable, and the one acre lot of land they were using for garden. They were guaranteeing the right to use the pump on the main farm, the right to walk on the property, and right to be medically provided for. They were guaranteeing care in the older years.

That they were using this one acre for a garden seems to be evident in the will when it states "the said Jacob S. Metzler, his heirs and assigns, shall, annually furnish one two-horse load of good manure, and to be hauled by him, on the said lot of one acre of land, for their use." The manure would have made the perfect fertilizer.

The 1875 map of West Earl shows two buildings across from one another, both owned by Jacob S. Metzler. The buildings on the 1864 and 1875 maps noted places of dwelling. So why are there not two dwellings marked on the 1864 map? Here is a guess: the 1864 atlas has Jacob Metzler, presumedly Jacob H. Metzler as still owning the farm. Again it is not officially deeded off until 1865. The 1875 map clearly notes the farm is now owned by Jacob S. Metzler, his son. The second dwelling house appears because Jacob H. and his wife are probably living in the 16 by 13 by this time. The 81 on the 1875 map is for acreage owned,

A photo from the early 1900s: John S. Metzler is on the left, Christian M. Hess, his nephew is in the middle, and Samuel S. Metzler is on the right. The woman in the photo was trying to get out of the camera shot. The photo was taken at the Hess farm near Rothsville, PA. Photo courtesy of Joann Metzler Herr (John S. Metzler was her great grandfather).

apparently owned by Jacob S. Metzler.

The one acre of improved land and 18 acres of unimproved land were probably never officially deeded off, but rather more of a contractual agreement between father and son.

John S. Metzler's Farm

Jacob H. Metzler sold John S. Metzler, Jacob S. Metzler's twin brother, the adjacent 74 acre farm to the west on June 13, 1859 for $3750 dollars. John died October 31, 1921 due to a cold that developed into pneumonia. He was described as a man of an unassuming and kindly disposition and a pleasant conversationalist. He was actively involved in the Metzler's Mennonite congregation, leading singing when the services were mostly in German.[14]

A 1950 ariel photo of the John S. Metzler farm. Courtesy of Jane Metzler Zimmerman.

The Passing of Jacob H. Metzler

Jacob H. Metzler passed away on April 23, 1878; Barbara died one year later, on November 23, 1879.

Following their deaths, a second sale took place on December 18th, 1879, executed by Jacob S. Metzler and his twin brother, John. Items sold included:

a rockaway sleigh	harness
fly net	ax and saws
3 beds and steads	kitchen dresser
fly net	ax and saws
a desk	corner and other cupboards
chests	tables
stands	chairs
rocking chairs	sofa

clock	meal chest
cooking stove	parlor cook and pipe
a sink	one ton of coal
buffalo robe	copper and iron kettles
barrels,	barrel and vinegar
kegs	apple butter by the crock
potatoes	tubs
pot rack	carpet by the yard
grub	hoes
shovels	spades
tin	earthen and queens ware
rifle	mirrors
oil cloth	a lot of books

How This Connects to the Hertzog Homestead

Jacob H. Metzler deeded off the land so that Metzler's Meetinghouse could be established. He converted the one story stone dwelling into the two story federalist style house that exists today. He installed the corner cupboard and the Indian door as well. He also tore down part of the southern barn gable and lengthened to barn to accommodate newer farm machinery and provide him with more storage space. Under him the farm grew to it greatest breath of 153 acres.

The Jacob H. Metzler Family Tree

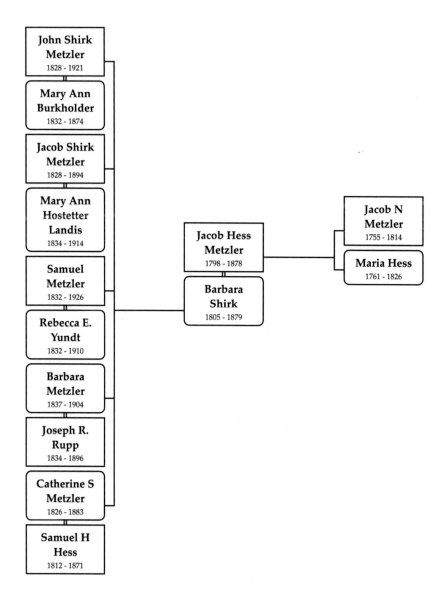

PUBLIC SALE.

ON THURSDAY, DECEMBER 18th, 1879,

Will be sold at the late residence of Jacob Metzler, deceased, about 1 1-4 miles north of Farmersville, and near Metzler's Meeting House, in West Earl Twp., the following personal property, to wit:

1 ROCKAWAY,

Sleigh, Harness, Fly Net, Ax, Saws,

3 BEDS AND STEADS,

KITCHEN-DRESSER,

Corner and other Cupboards,

DESK, CHESTS,

TABLES, STAND, CHAIRS, ROCKING CHAIRS,

SOFA, CLOCK, MEAL CHEST, COOKING STOVE,

Parlor Cook and Pipe, about one ton of Coal, Sink,

Copper and Iron Kettles, Buffalo Robe, Barrel and Vinegar, Barrels, Kegs, Apple Butter by the Crock, Potatoes, Tubs, Stands, Carpet by the yard, Pot Rack, Grub Hoe, Shovel, Spade, Hoes, Tin, Earthen and Queens-ware, Rifle, Mirrors, Oil Cloth, a lot of Books, and many articles too numerous to mention.

Sale to commence at 1 o'clock P. M. of said day. Terms made known, by

**JOHN METZLER,
JACOB S. METZLER,**

Dec. 4th, 1879.   H. S. Hoffman, auct.   Executors of said deed

Printed at E. H. Burkholder's Job-printing Office, Farmersville, Pa.

The 1879 Sale Bill

Jacob S. Metzler:
Civil War and Tobacco

A Family Divided

When the Confederate States fired on Fort Sumter on April 12, 1861, beginning the American Civil War, it not only divided a nation, but also a family.

Jacob S. Metzler tethered his horse to the rail outside the US Postal Office. He tightened the quick release knot and strode toward the front door of the Brownstown Post Office. He pulled out the Conscientious Objector form from his shirt pocket. As devout member of the Metzler Society of Mennonites, this was a non issue for him. He would not fight, and believed that Christ had called him to a life of peace. He ascribed the "non-resistant doctrine of the Gospel", upholding the sentiments of the "Rules and Doctrine of the Lancaster Conference".

His twin brother John was exempt from enlisting with the Northern Armies due to his children, but if he would have had to, Jacob knew his brother would have registered as a Conscientious Objector as well. But their younger brother Samuel took a different position on military service.

After Samuel married Rebecca, they moved to Chicago, where Samuel worked as a veterinary surgeon. But his brother no longer held to the Anabaptist beliefs with which the Metzler family had been raised. He supported the war effort of the North, believing that God had called for the the freedom of slaves, not only spiritually, but also physically. Though Samuel was distant, his actions were the source of some tension and discussion around the evening table in Jacob's house. Samuel's father was not happy. It would become even a greater discussion when Samuel decided to join up with the 17th Illinois Calvary on January 22, 1864.

Jacob S. Metzler Takes Over the Plantation

By 1860, Jacob S. Metzler inherited the family farm of 77 acres, with a total of 74 acres of improved land and 3 acres of unimproved land valued at $9600. By 1875, he added an

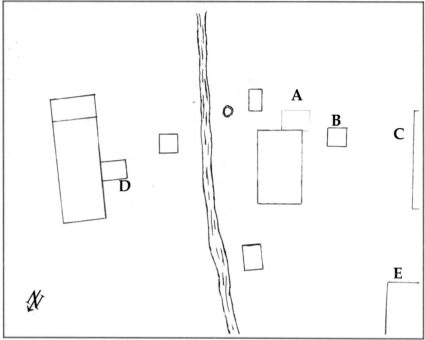

A. Summer kitchen is added to the main house in the 1880s. B. A shed, likely for storage, was probably built during Jacob S. Metzler's era, though it could potentially have been built by his father. C. In response to Lancaster County's growing tobacco industry, a tobacco shed is built on the property. D. An extension is built out the front of the barn to provide more tobacco and hay storage. E. Jacob S. Metzler's retirement house is built.

additional 4 acres.[1] Like his father, farming seemed to be going well for him. He and Mary Ann Landis had no children at the time, so it is not surprising he had hired help. They had four hired hands living with them in the farmhouse: a farm laborer named Harrison Fronkhouser, Ann Eliza Landis (possibly a relative of Mary Ann), a laborer named Augustus Hoy, and his brother Francis Hoy.

His father made sure Jacob was provided for and helped him establish the farm. He gave him an advancement (pictured on the following page) of 2 horses, 1 mare, horse gears, collars, bridles, and a flynet. He also advanced him a plow, spreader, a set of hay ladders, and a windmill. Many other cattle, farm implements, and house furnishings were given as well.[2]

144

Advancement Made
To My Son Jacob

		$	c
1	Horse	100	00
1	Desk	25	00
1	Bed & bedstead	18	00
1	Bible	7	00
1	Horse	28	00
1	Mare	25	00
1	Wagon	18	00
1	Windmill	10	00
8	Flone years	8	00
2	Collars at 50 cts each	3	00
3	Bridles .. 50	1	50
3	Halders . the lot	1	75
1	Fly net	0	50
1 pair Brest chair		0	93¾
1 u Tracers		0	43¾
1	Plow	3	10
1 pair Hay ladders		4	00
1	Spreaders	1	00
1	Line		62½
1st set Hay ladders		2	75
		252	12

Continued

		$	
1 Broad Wheeled Wagon with bed bows Cover & feed trough		65	00
1	Calf	3	00
1	Heaffer	8	00
1	Cow	15	00
1	Fork	0	50
4	Cow Chains	1	30
2	Log Chaines	3	12½
1 Small Shovel Harrow		0	12½
1	Cart	2	00
1 ten plate Stove & pipe		7	50
1	Table	1	62½

Also with advancement made to him, in the land
which I sold and conveyed to him, and so more
showed in his Deed ———— $1700.00

$2060.00

1860 Tax records show that Jacob S. owned 6 horses, 4 milch cows, 7 other cattle, and 28 swine valued at $700.00. Swine were raised in the pole barn between the Sweitzer barn and the house. Jacob S. also had farm machinery valued at $250 dollars, some of which came from the advancement from his father. One of these items was a windmill, which would have stood near the hand dug well. In addition, he also had 500 bushels of wheat (stored in the granary), 5 bushels of rye, 200 bushels of Indian corn, 200 bushels of Oats, 20 bushels of Irish Potatoes, 6 bushels of sweet potatoes, orchard products valued at $10.00, 300 pounds of butter, and 30 tons of hay. He, like his father, slaughtered animals, with them being valued at $150 dollars.

Jacob S. Metzler's Children

In 1861, Jacob S. and Mary Ann welcomed their first child, Elizabeth Landis Metzler, on May 22. She later married Daniel W. Buch and they eventually took up residence the Plantation. She was my great, great grandmother. Four years later, John Landis Metzler was born on October 7. He lived to be 6 years old. His cause of death is unknown. The third and last child of Jacob S. and Mary Ann was born on July 15th, 1869. Her name was Barbara Landis Metzler. Barbara married Jacob N. Stoner in September of 1918, when she was 49 years of age and he was 67. Jacob N. Stoner, who was born on November 15, 1851, died on December 20, 1927. After Jacob Stoner's death, she married Samuel K. Landis. She never had any children. She took my grandmother, her niece under her wing, and they were close.

The Farm's Prosperity

1870 tax records list Jacob S. Metzler as a farmer, owning 81 acres of improved land, valued at $16,000 dollars. His personal property was valued at $3,000 dollars. Mary Ann is listed as keeping house. He had one hired hand: Henry Springer. At this time, the plantation held 7 horses, 6 milch cows, 8 other cattle, and 9 swine (down from the 28 he had 10 years prior). These were valued at $900.00. His farm machinery was valued at $200 dollars, and he had paid $300 dollars in wages. That he was paying wages is not surprising. His children in 1870 would have been very young and unable to help him on the farm. He would have needed help harvesting his crops,

Barbara Metzler in her twenties.

An 1873 American Education Reader No. 5 that belonged to Barbara Metzler when she attended school at the Metzler's one room school house.

Above: Barbara Metzler and Samuel K. Landis on the John S. Metzler Farm
Below: Barbara Metzler on the right; her sister Lizzie Metzler is on the left.

slaughtering his animals, and making his butter.

According to oral tradition, John B. Weaver, the great-grandfather to Diamond Station resident Harvey Weaver, worked for Jacob S. Metzler as one such laborer. Born in 1858, he worked for Jacob in the late 1870s or early 1880s. He traveled from Juniata County, Pennsylvania where he lived to Lancaster to work because he could get higher wages as a hired boy for Jacob earning

A 1950's ariel photo of the Tobacco shed.

$11.00 month. Some of his work might have included throwing wheat for storage on top of the third story beams in the barn.

The plantation farm was producing well. Jacob harvested over 500 bushels of winter wheat, 700 bushels of Indian Corn, 400 Bushels of Oats, 30 bushels of Irish Potatoes, and orchard products valued at $120 dollars. In addition to that, his family made 700 pounds of butter, brought in 20 tons of hay, and slaughtered animals valued at $434.00. The total value of the farm production was $2890.00.[3] This is about $97,139.73 in 2016.

The Plantation Under Jacob Metzler

What was the farm like under Jacob S. Metzler? After his death, Mary Ann had a sale on September 6th, 1894 that consisted of non-household goods. She sold things like:

shovel harrow   apple butter by the crock

149

quarrying tools	a lot of carpenter tools
cross-cut saw	two stoves
a buggy	a tabacco wagon
a spring wagon	tobacco ladders
1200 tobacco lath	vinegar by the barrel

Jacob S. Metzler clearly raised acres of tobacco. He was probably continuing a tradition started by his father, who had lengthened the barn to accommodate more tobacco. Jacob S. Metzler built a tobacco shed, allowing him to increase the volume of his tobacco production. Tobacco remained a core crop for the next two generations of the plantation's inhabitants.

Tobacco sheds began to appear in Lancaster County somewhere after 1865. It was soon after this that Jacob S. Metzler most likely built his.

The September 6, 1894 Sale Bill

Pennsylvania cigar filler and binder leaf required air-curing. Air-curing required cadding, ventilation boards on the side of the shed, that could open and close to regulate the curing. The picture on page 162 shows these open on the tobacco shed that Jacob S. Metzler built. The tobacco cellar, or dampening room, was at the southern end of the shed beside the field. This extended halfway underneath and was used for stripping and baling.[4]

The plantation under Jacob S. Metzler continued to have a fairly large orchard. This allowed him to produce and sell barrels of vinegar and crocks of apple butter.

Jacob continued quarrying stone and cutting lumber. He, like his ancestors, probably pulled the stone from the fields and from the farm quarry which bordered his brother's property. This was used in the foundations of the summer kitchen, the retirement house he later built, and to help build the tobacco cellar.

The Hospitality of Jacob S. Metzler

The 1880 census shows that Jacob S. and Mary Ann have a servant named Simon Shirk, who was a relative of his mother's. Prior to this, his twin brother's wife died on September 1, 1874, leaving his brother John to raise 8 children. Jacob and Mary Ann helped out and assumed guardianship of the youngest child, David, who was five.[5] They took responsibility for him until 1890, when he turned 21. David eventually assumed responsibility of his father's farm.

A young David Metzler

Jacob's Retirement House

As 1890 approached, Jacob S. Metzler was thinking of retirement. His father had retired around the age of 60, so it makes sense that as he now approached that age, he considered doing the same thing. Perhaps because he was financially able and

The two story frame house as it exists in 2013.

perhaps because he did not want to live in the log summer house, he decided to build a two story frame house for him and his wife to retire in. It was finished by 1888 when he insured it on a Mennonite Mutual Aid document. About 10 years later after its first official mention on this insurance document, his twin brother John built a retirement house in 1898 just west of High Road. The date 1898 appears on a board in the attic of John's house. The floor plan mirrored the frame house Jacob built. As with his twin brother Jacob, John apparently thought of his house as a retirement house.

When Jacob S. Metzler finished building his retirement house, he moved into it along with his wife and unmarried daughter Barbara. Lizzie, who married Daniel Buch in 1884, moved into the main plantation house with her new husband. The whole farm, however, remained under Jacob's ownership until his death in 1894. At that point the main farm of 50 acres was deeded to Lizzie and 32 acres was given to Barbara. After he died, Mary Ann and Barbara remained in the retirement house.

One final thing about Jacob Metzler's retirement house. Apparently on April 3, 1908, a spark from a traction engine ignited a straw stack and burned the entire stack to the ground. No injuries were reported.[6]

The Summer Kitchen

Jacob S. Metzler added a summer kitchen to the main plantation house right around the time he built his retirement home. Stylistically it matches the construction of the house he built across the street. An 1889 Insurance document mentioned a two story stone house insured with its attachments. Was one such attachment the summer kitchen, with its ground cellar below and bedroom above? It seems likely. All other buildings on the farm are listed separately. As a side note, the original German siding still exists underneath the layer of insulation and vinyl siding that Kenneth and Arlene Hertzog, my parents and future owners, placed over it.

1976 picture of the summer kitchen with the German wood siding exposed.

The summer kitchen was designed to make living in the plantation house more comfortable. Sometime in April or May, the family would move the kitchen out of the main house and into the summer kitchen, where they would cook, take their meals, and can and preserve food. When September and October came, they would move the kitchen back into the main house, closing off the summer kitchen for the winter. The two foot stone walls kept the main house warmer in the winter. When the summer heat persisted, the main house became quite stuffy inside. The summer kitchen helped alleviate this.

Jacob S. Metzler's Death

Jacob S. Metzler died on April 3, 1894, at 5:15 PM, a death brought on by Bright's disease (a disease that caused inflammation of the kidneys), which had developed in the Christmas of 1893. At this time, he was confined to the plantation house with rheumatism, probably living on the first floor due to the pain in his joints. Until that time, he was always described as robust and was almost never sick. Neighbors liked him, and said he was a quality man of both heart and mind. The funeral at Metzler's Meetinghouse was conducted in German by Reverend Elias Nolt and Joseph Wenger and in English by Jacob N. Brubacher.[7]

Mary Ann, his wife, died on January 12, 1914. She was not able to walk the last year of her life and was confined to her bed most of the time, her mind and body being weak. She apparently never complained.[8]

How This Connects to the Hertzog Homestead

Jacob S. Metzler built the summer kitchen and the retirement house that his wife and daughter eventually lived in. They both still exist today. After he died, thirty acres were attached to the retirement house and it was deeded to his wife. Because of the tobacco boom in Lancaster County, he built the tobacco shed that is evident in pictures from the 1950s and 1960s.

The Jacob Shirk Metzler Family Tree

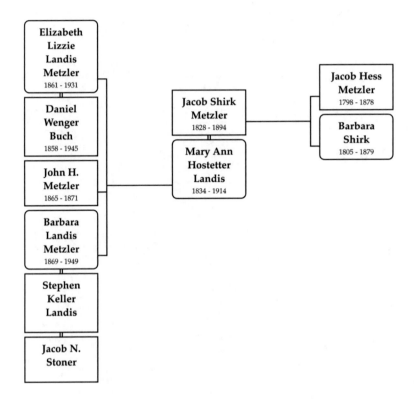

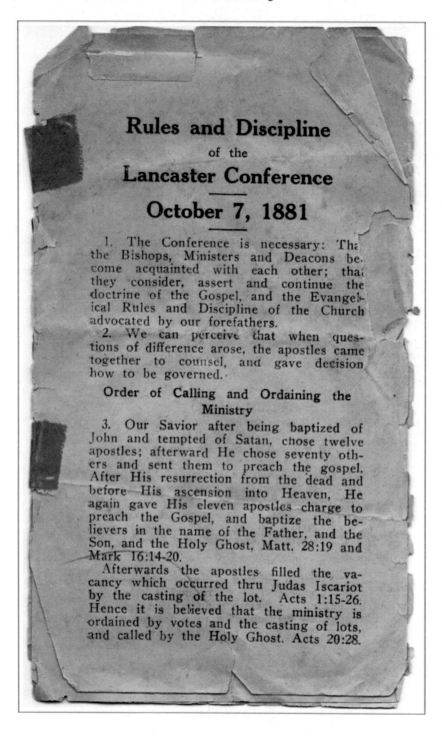

Rules and Discipline

of the

Lancaster Conference

October 7, 1881

1. The Conference is necessary: Tha; the Bishops, Ministers and Deacons become acquainted with each other; thai they consider, assert and continue the doctrine of the Gospel, and the Evangelical Rules and Discipline of the Church advocated by our forefathers.

2. We can perceive that when questions of difference arose, the apostles came together to counsel, and gave decision how to be governed.

Order of Calling and Ordaining the Ministry

3. Our Savior after being baptized of John and tempted of Satan, chose twelve apostles; afterward He chose seventy others and sent them to preach the gospel. After His resurrection from the dead and before His ascension into Heaven, He again gave His eleven apostles charge to preach the Gospel, and baptize the believers in the name of the Father, and the Son, and the Holy Ghost, Matt. 28:19 and Mark 16:14-20.

Afterwards the apostles filled the vacancy which occurred thru Judas Iscariot by the casting of the lot. Acts 1:15-26. Hence it is believed that the ministry is ordained by votes and the casting of lots, and called by the Holy Ghost. Acts 20:28.

The apostles commanded that the Church shall always be provided with Bishops, Ministers and Deacons.

Choosing the Ministry

4. The counsel of the Church is taken; if favorable, then votes shall be taken.

The brethren who receive votes having the qualifications of I Tim. 3:1-13, and Titus 1:6-9 shall pass through the lot.

The Ministry shall not be salaried.

The Duties of the Ministry

5. It is the duty of the Bishop to instruct and baptize the penitent believer, and to receive such into the church, with the counsel of the Church; to hold communion and feetwashing with them; to excommunicate the disobedient, with the Word and counsel of the Church.

6. It is the duty of the Minister to preach the Word of God, warn sinners, to comfort the penitent and to point them to faith in Jesus. A minister shall not baptize except in case of sickness, when the service of a Bishop cannot be secured at the time.

7. It is the duty of a Deacon to distribute to the poor members of the Church, to read the text for the Minister in the meeting if requested. In case no minister is present in the meeting, the Deacon shall read a portion of scripture and pray with the congregation.

When enmity arises in the Church, the Deacon shall look after it.

Receiving Believers into the Church

8. They shall be examined if they are at peace, are penitent and believing, and are willing to submit wholly to the Evangelical, non-resistant doctrine of the Gos-

2

157

pel, and to the rules of the Church, wherein they shall be fully and plainly instructed before baptism and shall be received into the Church, with the counsel of the Church.

Order in the Church

9. The Church consists of penitent believing and obedient members

10. The Church shall be examined, before the Communion, to learn if the members are at peace; at which service it is customary to preach on the 18th chapter of Matthew.

11. A day of fasting and prayer is observed before Communion.

12. Feetwashing is observed immediately after Communion

13. When grievances, or differences arise between members, the grieved members shall observe Matt. 18.

No Bishop, Minister or Deacon shall receive a complaint before the brotherly address according to Matthew 18:13-18 has been complied with.

14. When a member commits a wrong against any person out of the church, or an open transgression, the complainant shall examine the report as to its truth, before he brings the matter before the ministry.

15. When a member absents himself (or herself) from Communion and does not support the Church, then such members shall be visited and examined If he is unable to attend to his duties as a member he shall be borne in patience and love. But if he can and will not, then he shall be visited several times and admonished, and if he still refuses, then he shall be given over to the Church.

3

Change of Location

16. When members move from one bishop district to another, they shall present
letters of standing from the congregation
from which they came.

When a bishop, minister or deacon
moves from his appointed field to another,
his ministry shall not be recognized, until
the congregation where he locates shall
call for such recognition, ad then only
by the consent of the congregation from
which he came, and with the consent of
Conference.

When such change is made from one
Conference to another such call shall be
made from one Conference to the other.

Matrimony

17. We acknowledge a Christian marriage between one man and one woman
who are believers and lead a non-resistant
life The nuptials shall be announced in
Church. If a member marries outside of
the Non-conforming Churches that member is back from Communion and Council
of Brethren until he acknowledges that
he has transgressed the Evangelical discipline of the Church

Such a member can be reinstated by a
Bishop. If a member marries one who is
divorced, such member forfeits membership so long as the former partner is living; then can be reinstated. Anyone
married to one divorced cannot be received into the Church as long as the
former partner is living

Only a Bishop shall solemnize the marriage of members and the ministers those
only who are not members, the Ministers
subject to the Bishops. Each Bishop to
officiate in his own district.

When members engage a minister of
some other denomination in preference to

4

their own, to solemnize their marriage, they fall under censure.

Wedding marches and flower girls are not allowed when members marry.

The Lord's Day Observance

18. The Lord's day should be well observed by God's people and make it a day of devotion and worship. Church service and Sunday school should be regularly attended. Feasting and pleasure seeking should be strictly avoided Both young and old should be taught how to keep the Lord's day holy and exercise themselves constantly in showing reverence to God's house and all that pertains thereto.

Protracted Meetings

19. They are approved providing the "bench" agrees and the council of the church is favorable. Such meetings to be subject to conference. The evangelists who conduct those meetings shall be selected from the body of this conference with the consent of the bishop or any other evangelist may be selected who has been approved by the board of bishops of Lancaster conference.

Conference does not approve of any bishop or minister working in any district contrary to the rules of conference or labor without the consent of the bishop or ministry.

Lay members are not allowed to engage bishops or ministers and make appointments for them.

Sunday Schools

20. Conference recommends that Sunday schools shall be held, and shall be conducted subject to Conference.

5

Members shall be selected for teachers as much as possible.

Superintendents shall be consistent, communicant members strictly in order, also the teachers.

Conference does not approve of Sunday school libraries, except brethren authorized by Conference, would select a library free from fiction.

Members are not allowed to be members of the Young Men's Christian Association nor Epworth League nor Christian Endeavor. Members are not allowed to take part in revivals held by those who do not uphold and practice the non-resistant doctrine of the Gospel.

Pride

21. "That which is highly esteemed among men is abomination in the sight of God." Jesus says, "Learn of me, for I am meek and lowly in heart." Conference does require that Bishops, Ministers and Deacons, their wives (the wives being members) shall conform to the order of the Church and earnestly admonish the lay members to do the same. If members become proud and vain they fall under censure. It is not allowed to put flowers on the remains of members. It is advised members shall not allow flowers to be put on the remains of their family.

Worldly Amusements

22 Excursion parties, surprise parties, camping-out parties by unmarried members, entertainments, all public contests in games, attending circuses, movies, theaters helping to arrange for and attending festivals, fairs, picnics, literary societies, buying and selling of tickets of chance,— these as well as all other amusements of a similar character are forbidden.

6

Swearing of Oaths

23. Our communication shall be Yea, Yea; Nay Nay; Matt. 5. According to the non-resistant doctrine of the Gospel it is not allowed to take the sword, nor to sue at law. If any member sues at the law he is put back from Council of Brethren and Communion, until he acknowledges that he has transgressed the Gospel.

24. Conference does not approve of Members serving in any worldly office whatever, but would earnestly advise them to keep out of those offices, and if they sue at law they fall under censure as in Art. 23.

Secret Societies

25. All secret societies, Life-insurance, and Theft Insurance, are forbidden.

Members are not allowed to belong to labor-unions.

Serving as Jurors

26. When a murderer is on trial, it is forbidden, but is allowed in other cases. It is however advised that members shall avoid it as much as possible.

Regulations for Conference and Mission Board

27. The bishops shall meet together Thursday morning, before Conference to give the Ministry an opportunity to bring before them matters wherein they need advice.

Brethren who desire advice or who have a matter to bring before conference shall present the same in writing before the board of bishops.

The board of missions and charities shall present a report of their work to the board of bishops for approval.

Every decision made by conference shall

7

be written out and copies given to the
ministers who desire them

The bishops shall unanimously agree before they bring any decision before conference for ratification.

Every decision made by the bishops
shall be ratified by two-thirds of conference, voting, before the same shall be
announced to the churches as a rule of
conference.

When less than fifty members of conference vote the question shall be considered tabled.

Only ministers and deacons shall vote
at conference.

Appealing to Conference

28. When enmity or strife occurs in
one Bishop's district, no Bishop, Minister
or Deacon shall meddle therewith, unless
called by said Bishop. In case, however
a Bishop should teach wrong doctrines
contrary to the non-resistant doctrine, or
lead his congregation astray, then his congregation can appeal to Conference.

Violations of Conference Rules

29. If any member shall wilfully and
knowingly violate the rules of Conference,
such offending member shall be visited
and the matter investigated, and if the
charge be found true, he shall be requested
to come before the Church, acknowledge
his error, and ask for forbearance. If he
refuses to do so, he shall be suspended
from Council of Brethren and Communion
until he is willing to do so.

When a member is put back from the
Church those members, who stand by such,
place themselves in the same state.

Rohrerstown, Lancaster Co., Pa.

March 22-23, 1923

Daniel and Lizzie Metzler Buch: Telephones, Trolleys, and Farming

Getting over
the old stile

Clear skies, green fields, full barns for
the farmer who appreciates that the old
order of things has passed.

To be modern is to have a Bell telephone.
To have a telephone is *to live*. Write
to-day for Rural line booklet.

Denver & Ephrata Tel & Tel Co.
C. E. Eaby, Mgr.   Ephrata, Pa.

The Amen Corner

Daniel Buch hunched down in the far corner of the wooden bench in the back of the "Amen Corner" in Metzler's Mennonite Church. His ledger lay open on his coarse black pants. He occasionally nodded as if paying attention to Joseph E. Wenger, the minister. John Sauder, the church custodian, sat next to him; come Monday, he would be helping Daniel run the thresher for the wheat harvest. The warm, muggy air in the brick church made it easy to nod off, but he avoided that by balancing his books.

Occasionally, he would glance up and catch the eye of Lizzie, his wife, who sat on the ladies' side of the church, and her stern look and frown would cause him to duck his head down again. He justified what he was doing. After all, he was the treasurer for the church. So what if he occasionally balanced farm books as well?

The Buchs Arrive on the Plantation

Elizabeth Landis Metzler, known as Lizzie, married financier Daniel Wenger Buch on November 27, 1884. He was

Daniel Buch's parents: Jacob R. Buch and Mary W. Wenger

born on March 9, 1858, and was the son of Jacob R. Buch and Mary Wenger. Many Buch farms dotted the landscape between Brownstown, PA and Akron, PA. Daniel Buch grew up on a farm just south of Akron, PA on what now is Eagle View Estates. After Daniel and Lizzie were married, they moved onto the plantation and Jacob, Mary Ann, and Barbara Metzler moved into Jacob's retirement house across the street. After Lizzie's father died, the main farmstead was deeded to her in 1896. Her sister Barbara and her mother continued living in the retirement house. Barbara lived there with her mother Mary Ann until her mother died in 1914.

When the retirement house was deeded to Mary Ann and Barbara in 1896, the property had no barn and contained only 32 acres. Although late in the 1880s he had divided the property, Jacob clearly viewed this as one property[1]; it was farmed as one farm. Jacob and Daniel farmed together until Jacob's death and used the same barn, the Swietzer barn, on the main plantation property. A barn does appear on the property in 1899.[2] After Jacob's death, Daniel Buch continued farming the entirety of both properties, most likely paying rent and making sure that his mother-in-law and sister-in-law were provided for. This would have been in the tradition of Jacob S. and Jacob H. and how they provided for the widows in the family. They thus upheld the scripture "if a widow has children or grandchildren, these should learn first of all to put their religion into practice by caring for their own family and so repaying their parents and grandparents" 1 Timothy 5:4 (NIV). Jacob B. Metzler, son of John S. Metzler, also helped harvest crops on Mary Ann's and Barbara's farm.[3]

Late 19th Century Mennonite Weddings

On Thursday, November 27th, 1884, Daniel Buch of Akron, PA, dressed in his best suit. As he stepped out onto the porch of his father's house, he looked south toward the Jacob Metzler Plantation in the distance and smiled. His bride-to-be waited a short carriage ride away. He stepped off the porch and walked toward the carriage; his younger brother Jacob W. Buch stood at the horse's head, keeping the carriage steady as the animal neighed and huffed in the cold November air. It was Thanksgiving Day, and he had much to be thankful for.

A short ride later, he stepped down in front of Elizabeth Metzler's house. He fished his pocket watch out of his breast pocket; the time was 9 am. In just an hour, at 10 am, he would be married to his sweetheart here on the Plantation. He stepped up to the front porch and was

1884 Daniel and Lizzie Buch Wedding Photo

greeted by E. S. Brownsmiller, the Lutheran Minister, who would perform the wedding ceremony. He nodded a greeting to Barbara Metzler Hess and Mary Burkholder Metzler, who were official witnesses to the ceremony. They were Lizzie's first cousins. A few other family friends gathered as well.[4]

As was customary of the times, Daniel and Lizzie were not yet baptized members of Metzler's Mennonite Church; therefore, the minister of their church could not marry them. According to historian Ira D. Landis, it was quite common for Lutheran ministers to be the defacto clergymen in such cases, a practice that ran from the early-1700s until the late 1880s.[5]

Buch Life on the Homestead

Daniel and Lizzie had three children: Jacob Metzler Buch was born on October 27, 1885, Harry Metzler Buch was born on February 25, 1887, and Elmer Metzler Buch was born on March 15, 1891.

It is at this point in history that we begin to get some photographic evidence, depicting what life must have been like on the farm. One such photo depicts the family sawing wood, the main heating source for the house along with coal, and used perhaps to kindle the lime kiln.

Another picture shows them threshing wheat or rye on the hill south of the original Jacob Metzler Plantation, most likely taken sometime in the 1920s. An old Ford truck can been seen in this photograph. While it looks to be the same truck pictured at the Elmer Metzler Buch's sale later on in

Jacob Metzler Buch

Jacob M. Buch and Harry M. Buch Metzler School Picture Circa 1890s. Elmer is first to the left in the first row; Jacob and Harry are first to the left in the second row.

The Buchs sawing wood.

The Buchs Threshing

Harry, Elmer, and Jacob Metzler Buch

this book, it is not. Next to it is a tobacco steamer that is powering the bulky threshing machine. There are bags of grain in front of the threshing machine. A pipe snakes down the side filling bags of grain as some men work the baling part of the threshing machine and stacking the bales on on the wagon.

On Account of Daniel Buch

An 1889 - 1909 account book tells us a bit about life for Daniel and Lizzie when they first took over the farmstead. For example, we know in 1894 he paid Jacob Genemer, Heiram Evans, Monroe Mellinger for help with hay making, harvesting, thrashing, corn shelling, coating dung, and plowing. He also rented horses to help with plowing. In the subsequent years, John Sauder, trustee at Metzler's Mennonite Church, also was enlisted to help with haymaking and harvesting.

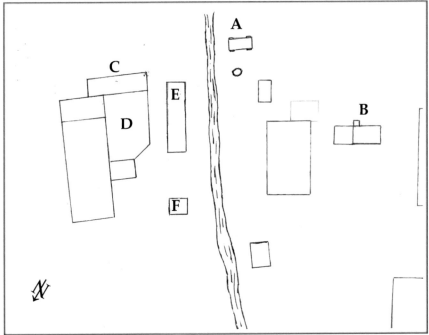

A. Rolling machine shed built, initially used to store equipment. B. A chicken house is added onto shed. This allies with Lancaster County's growing chicken industry. An outhouse/privy is also sketched here. Potentially exists earlier than Daniel Buch's era. C. A block machine shop is built. D. The barnyard probably existed in the same location prior to this time; however, Daniel Buch built the block walls that hem in the barnyard today. E. Carriage house is extended to add a car garage at one end, and machine storage at the other. The center portion is used to raise pigs. F. A second garage is built, most likely to house Jacob or Elmer's cars.

That he rented horses and hired day laborers to help with the harvest made sense. His oldest son would have been 13 at time with his other sons not yet reaching the age of 10. And this sharing of resources was common. He assisted neighboring farmers and rented three of his horses out to them as well to help with threshing.

His accounts show that he sold winerger (vinegar), potatoes for eating, and potatoes for seed. He sold John Sauder, who lived in the Elias Meyer Miller's house, beef, hogs, and pudding (fried up and made of livers, hearts and the meat from a hog's head) in a crock. It also shows that he had wheat ground into flour by Samuel Rupp at Rupp's Mill, who was mentioned earlier in this book. This meant he raised wheat.

The account books also tells us some of the items he bought. He bought steers from Jacob B. Zwally in Akron. From Elam Irvin he bought suspenders, a straw hat, 3 pairs of socks, one pair of overalls, and shoes.

The Great Blizzard of 1895

When the great blizzard of February 1895 hit, it shut down all train and trolley service. Over six to ten feet of snow blanketed the county with the 60 mile an hour winds creating 20 foot drifts.[6] Daniel helped his neighbors by shoveling snow on February 15, 18, and 20, for which he received payment. He even charged for the use of his horses and the snow tack.[7]

The Great Blizzard of 1895

An early 1900's McCormick Deering Grain Binder

Farming in the Early 1900s

The inventory list at Daniel's death tells that he raised hay for 19 steers (8 of which averaged 875 pounds and were valued at $.13 a pound and 11 which averaged 1100 pounds and averaged $. 115 per pound). He had

a hay loader	side delivery rake
a horse mower	a manure spreader
one mule	a McCormick Deering Grain Binder
a cultivator	2 New Idea farm wagons
a steel tank wagon	

He continued to raise tobacco and housed pigs in the long, narrow pole shed between the house and the barn.

The Summer of 1920

In the summer of 1920, J. Landis Weaver was hired out to Lizzie Buch when he was ten years of age, to teach him responsibility. He was living on the corner of Bethany and North Farmersville Road and would ride his bicycle two miles to the Buch farm, where he would eat breakfast and lunch. He was paid 25 cents a day.[8]

He would often arrive on the Buch farm after breakfast was over and his eggs had become cold. Lizzie had made his eggs by frying them in lard. He would eat them with bread and milk in the summer kitchen as he sat next to the cream separator, which, due to the smell, was not the ideal location for breakfast.

His job on the farm was to help Lizzie with the housework. This included washing dishes, cleaning, and running errands. He also mowed and trimmed the lawn and worked in the garden.

He makes mention of spending time looking at farm magazines on a screened in back porch. He may have been referring to what I always knew as the side porch. In my memory, it was never screened in. He describes Lizzie as a heavy woman, and that she seemed to have had bad feet.

He tells of two stories in his autobiography which I will share verbatim.

One hot day Dan, Liz's husband, was working in the west cornfield. Liz said to me, "I'll make some lemonade and you can take some out to Dan." Of course she had given me some, and I set out for the cornfield with a lard pail full of lemonade for Dan. It was very warm and the corn was tall. The rows of corn seamed endless. I took the lid off of the pail and sampled the lemonade. It was good; Soon I was thirsty again. I drank some more. Now I was afraid that Dan would ask me why Liz didn't fill the kettle, but he didn't. I think he knew!

On another day, I suppose she was tired of me hanging around. Liz said, "Go out and ask Dan if you can help him. He was in the field with a pair of mules hitched to the roller. Dan said, "Yes, you can walk after the roller and pick up small stones. At the end of   the field, you can give me a handful to throw at the mules." So all afternoon I walked through the dust after that roller and handed stones to Dan. I don't suppose that the mules minded one bit about the few stones that landed on their backs or flew past their ears. I guess Liz and Dan had a good laugh that evening.[9]

Inside the Buch House

Late in 1922 and into 1923, the neighborhood of farmers visted C.S.Wenger of Brownstown Electric, Light, Heat, and Power Company and began the process of bringing electric into the area. Up till this time, oil lamps lit the houses.[10]

We know a little bit about how the house was utilized and set up. On the first floor: we know that Daniel and Lizzie slept in the downstairs bedroom located in the northwestern room. The southwestern room was the kitchen. The living room was the northeastern room. The parlor was located in the southeastern room. The contents of the parlor were the highest valued on the inventory list at Daniel's death, suggesting that he displayed his valuables here. Daniel and Lizzie's bedroom had the second highest value.

The downstairs contained the summer kitchen with a wood stove in the little alcove that now contains the half-bath. There was no bathroom in the house, but the family used the privy to the west of the house. To get to the privy one would exit out the back door of the summer kitchen, cross a path, and arrive at the outhouse. The entrance to the hen house was behind this outhouse.

Each window of the plantation house had green window shades in them and had shutters on the outside that were closed in the summer to keep the house cool.

The upstairs rooms were used by Elmer and Jacob Metzler Buch, their sons. Most likely Harry also used one of the other two upstairs rooms, though because he no longer lived at home when Daniel died, it is difficult to tell which one. Elmer slept in the northeast bedroom with Jacob sleeping in the southwest bedroom, with a two doored wardrobe. The southeastern room was a spare room. Really this made sense. These were the only upstairs rooms with fireplaces built in. Also, Elmer's room was whitewashed. The hallways had carpet runners in them, something I remember from visiting the house when I was five, in 1975.[11]

Daniel Buch's Housekeeper: Annie Seibel

After Lizzie died in 1931, Daniel hired a housekeeper by the name of Annie Seibel, the widow of Israel Seibel. She worked for Daniel until she died in 1937 or 1938. Her granddaughter, Betty, sometimes would visit her, especially when her parents would go to a wedding or a funeral. Betty would often see Daniel sit on big chair next to a window; he barely spoke a word to her.

But Betty remembered helping her grandmother, "Mamie" as she called her, bake cookies. One time she give her some dough to prepare to make a pie, and it fell on the floor. Betty picked it up, but Mamie told her to throw it out because it was all covered with wood chips. It had fallen next to the wood box. The men who were coming in for lunch had a good laugh.[12]

Fire in the Washroom

On May 16, 1933, the only known fire burned on the homestead. A small wash house caught fire. Neighbors, perhaps John Metzler, Daniel Albright, and Martin Albright, helped to put out the blaze. In the end it destroyed $25 dollars worth of items, including the washing machine.[13] No one was hurt. We have no idea how much of the building was damaged.

The Trolley, Metzler's Station, and the Plantation

In the late 1800s, the electric street railway car, more commonly known as a trolley, became for many the ultimate means of travel. The Pennsylvania Traction Company, which placed many of the initial area trolley lines, declared bankruptcy in 1899 and was bought and and taken over by the Conestoga Traction Company.[14] In 1900, the Conestoga Traction Company commissioned the Lancaster, Mechanicsburg, and New Holland Railway Company to put in a trolley line from Mechanicsburg, which is now part of

The poles being put up along the old route

southwestern Leola, to Ephrata. Mechanicsburg was a clean and peaceful town and was once considered the business center of Earl Township. It derived its name from the mechanics and the machine shops that existed there.[15]

On April 14, Daniel Buch and John S. Metzler, the twin to

The trolley tracks in front of Conestoga Park

Jacob S. Metzler, made an agreement to allow the tracks to travel between their lands. They seem to have viewed the trolley not only as a financial gain, but also a sign of progress. They made final settlement on this in September.[16] Later that month, the poles were up, logged from local groves along the route. That October they, along with the other owners of the land on which the track was laid, were healthily reimbursed. Mid-October the engineers were preparing to bridge the Conestoga River

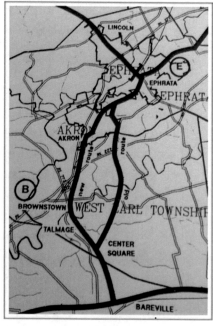

A map showing the old route, which passed by the Daniel Buch farm.

Top: The Diamond Station Trolley Station in the early 1900s and 2013. The waiting room was in this building. The station was once owned by the Rupp Family and later by the Andes Family.
Above: A view of the Diamond Station Trolley loading platform.
Left: Another view of the Diamond Station Trolley Station with a trolley waiting at the trolley platform. Old trolley photos courtesy of Jane Metzler Zimmerman.

Trolley Bridge at Conestoga Valley Park.

about a half mile away from Daniel and Lizzie's Farm. This work continued through November. By December, ties and iron rails were laid down.[17] The buttresses of this bridge can still be seen as can the trolley station in Diamond Station just down the road from Akron.

Why did the route not run through Talmage, Brownstown, and Akron? For example, Akron residents, if they wanted to take the trolley, had to walk almost a mile to Diamond Station to board it. The residents of these communities only had themselves to blame. When the Conestoga Traction Company first approached them about placing a trolley line through their town, the residents did not want these new-fangled cars running through and disturbing their communities.

By the middle of November, the grading was finished for the entire route, except in Ephrata and Mechanicsburg. There is some discrepancy as to whether the line officially opened in December of 1900 or March of 1901.[18] Whenever it did, one could ride from Ephrata to the east end of Lancaster for $.45.[19] The closest stations to the Daniel Buch farm were Metzler's Trolley Station[20], Diamond Station, and the Conestoga Valley Park Trolley Station.

The Conestoga Traction Company carried not only

passengers on their trolleys but freight as well, with packages stacked near the back of the car. Sometimes separate cars were used to haul stone and lumber. For example, the Conestoga Traction Company quarried stone off both Daniel Buch's and John S. Metzler's farms. This can be seen in the photos on prior pages. The bottom picture was taken facing south on Trolley Road, what now is High Road. The Lizzie Metzler farm is to the left. The top picture, perhaps taken the same day, shows trolley 51, along with a stone crushers, and was taken facing Daniel Buch's farm. It seems that another money maker on the farm would have been this quarried stone which would have been sold to the Conestoga Traction Company.

Akron, Brownstown, and Talmage apparently saw the error of their ways. They began a $350,000 dollar alteration of the current route, so costly because it required engineers to make deep cuts in the land, build some of the land up, and construct an immense metal bridge over the Conestoga River at Talmage. The work was completed by April 1924, bringing to an end the use of the four mile section that ran by the Daniel Buch farm. It really did make more sense for it to run through Akron, Talmage, and Brownstown since these communities were bigger and resulted in more revenue for the traction company.[21]

The last mention of the trolly line is pulled from line of an addendum to a deed, which allowed for the placement of pipes under the trolley line to drain water from the western side of the tracks onto the Lizzie Buch farm. Currently there are still pipes at this location. Actually it refers to the trolley line being now used

Put in deed of Lizzie Buch and husband to David Z. Hoover, dated April 15, 1926.

TOGETHER with the right to drain the water that collects on the west side of the embankment formed by the Ephrata & Adamstown Trolley Line, but which is now to be used as a driveway or lane, on land of the Grantors, by means of two terra or concrete pipes; said pipes not to be of greater diameter than 12 inches; and when new ones are replaced by the grantee, his heirs and assigns, they shall be placed where the present ones are, viz:, 13.45 perches and 29.7 perches, respectively, from the iron pin at the south end of the line bearing North thirteen degrees and fifty minutes West.

The Trolley Note

as a driveway or lane. The actual rails were removed sometime in the 1940s.

Sam Oberholtzer remembers in the late 1940s and early 1950s his father hiring Jack and Jim Mazer, who owned an excavating business, to push over the poles and fencing of the line that ran through his father's property so that they could farm it again.[22]

Denver and Ephrata Telephone and Telegraph

Daniel Buch was no mere farmer. He was an excellent financier and knew how to handle money. He helped finance the Denver and Ephrata Telephone and Telegraph Company's initial beginnings, and functioned as its treasurer, a job Jacob M. Buch, his son, eventually inherited. This eventually became D & E Communications, until it was bought by Windstream in November of 2009.

His account books, mentioned earlier, show him lending cash to people like John Yunginger, a practice his sons Jacob and Elmer would continue.

He owned stock in The Farmers Standard Carbide Company, Pennsylvania Power and Light, American Telephone and Telegraph Company, Consolidated Oil Corporation, Akron National Bank, Denver and Ephrata Telegraph and Telephone Company, and various bonds.

Recipes and Recollections

When my grandmother, Arlene Elizabeth Hertzog, the granddaughter of Daniel W. Buch, remembers Daniel, she remember him calling her Betsy, because of her middle name Elizabeth. Her middle name was after all the name of her grandmother and his wife. Lizzie would often pour coffee into a saucer to cool, so that my grandmother could drink it. She made

Above: Daniel W. Buch as the Treasurer in a 1920s D & E Board of Directors Meeting. He is third from the right. He co-contributed initial funding for the Denver and Ephrata Telephone and Telegraph Company start-up. Below: A posed picture of D & E's Board of Directors. Daniel is second from the left in the back row.

Above: Another picture of the board of directors of D & E. Daniel is second one from the right on the front row. Below: A picture of a board meeting from 1940. A much older looking Daniel Buch is seated second from the right. This photo was taken in the early 1940s.

Daniel W. Buch at the horse with his son Jacob M. Buch having a good laugh.

wonderful cakes with icing and would let her granddaughter lick the bowl.

We are lucky to have some of her recipes still with us. These may have been handed down from her mother.

Lizzie Metzler Buch's Roll Out Cookie
Ingredients:
2 cups of brown sugar
1 cup of shortening
3.5 cups of flour
2 teaspoons of baking powder
1 teaspoon of baking soda
.5 teaspoon of salt
2 eggs
2 tablespoons of water
1 teaspoon of vanilla

Directions:
Mix ingredients together; roll them out; cut them into shapes; brush them a little with beat up eggs; put on some sprinkles and then bake at 350 degrees until brown.

Lizzie Metzler Buch's Lemon Drop Cookies
Ingredients:
3 eggs
1 cup shortening
6 cups of flour (5 - 5.5 if Gold Medal)
3 teaspoons of lemon flavoring
3 cups of granular sugar
1 cup of sweet milk
3 teaspoons of baking soda

Directions:
Mix all ingredients thoroughly; then drop on a greased cookie sheet. Shake granulated sugar over the top and bake at 350 degrees for ten minutes or until firm. [23]

The Passing of Daniel and Lizzie Buch

Lizzie Metzler died before Daniel, at home, on December 10, 1931. A private service was held in the plantation house on Tuesday, December 15th at 1:30 with a public service following at Metzlers Mennonite Church. Daniel died at home as well on January 18, 1945. The farm was handed down to his sons, Jacob and Elmer Metzler Buch, both bachelors, in 1945.

How This Connects to the Hertzog Homestead

Daniel Buch was a good neighbor and ushered in the age of tractors and modern farm machinery on the farm. He did build the chicken house that stood behind the plantation house until the

1980s. He also had built the rolling machine shed that now serves as our chicken house.

The Daniel Wenger Buch Family Tree

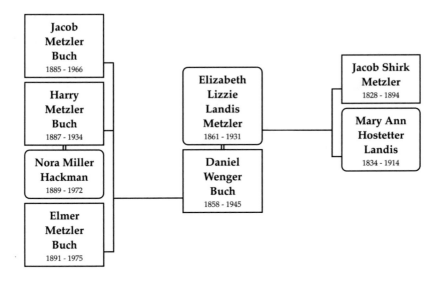

Jacob
Metzler
Buch
1885 - 1966

Harry
Metzler
Buch
1887 - 1934

Nora Miller
Hackman
1889 - 1972

Elmer
Metzler
Buch
1891 - 1975

Elizabeth
Lizzie
Landis
Metzler
1861 - 1931

Daniel
Wenger
Buch
1858 - 1945

Jacob Shirk
Metzler
1828 - 1894

Mary Ann
Hostetter
Landis
1834 - 1914

Jacob and Elmer Metzler Buch: Bachelor Life on the Plantation

Jacob M. Buch

Elmer M. Buch

K. Scott Hertzog

Beneath the Wheel

The John Deere H lumbered up the field, its plow digging straight furrows. It jostled Elmer to the sway of hardened earth and stubble from last year's harvest. An early May breeze blew around him, and he breathed it in deeply. He sighed. He loved this place. The farm. The land. The animals. The machinery. Especially the tractors. He had four others in the barn behind him. Being 73 years old, he walked with a cane, which now lay on the tractor's deck beneath his feet; it helped him climb onto the tractor. But once he was on the tractor, he was free and no longer confined by his limited mobility.

The tractor crested the hill and began to work its way down toward the edge of the field where the Buch land met Dan King's property. Elmer had marked the rows earlier with tobacco lath so that the rows he plowed would be neat and straight. He believed in precision farming. The tractor approached one of these markers now.

He leaned down between the tire and pully housing in order to pull the tobacco lath out of the ground and add to the stack he had already accumulated beside his cane. He pressed the clutch in as he always did slowing the tractor and plow to a stop.

As Elmer pulled the tobacco lathe out of the ground, his foot slipped off the clutch, releasing it. The tractor jerked forward. Elmer lost his grip on the steering wheel and fell against the wheel housing and then pitched forward in front the wheel. He felt the tractor's wheel and crushing weight roll over his upper thigh and felt the bones breaking. As the pain registered, he frantically reached up, his hand scrabbling for purchase on the axle moving by overhead. He did not want to be pulled beneath the blades of the plow. He pulled himself up with strength born out of desperation and crooked his arm around the axle. With his free hand, he grabbed the cane and used it to disengage the tractor. And then, in pain, he let himself fall to the hardened earth. He blacked out and lay unmoving.

Enos Horst was driving down West Metzler Road and saw the tractor out in the early afternoon sun. It struck him as odd. Being older gentlemen, Elmer and Jacob never plowed in the the heat of the day, preferring instead to plow in the mornings or late afternoon. Enos thought, "That tractor should not be out there at this time of day." Perhaps the tractor had broken down. Always willing to help out a neighbor and being fairly handy around tractors, he swung his truck into the Buch's driveway and drove out through the field.

And then he saw the body lying beneath the tractor. Something was wrong, horribly wrong. Bringing his truck to a halt, he leapt out and sprinted towards Elmer. He was not responsive, but had a pulse and was breathing. He ran back to his truck and wheeled it around. He drove to the main house, where he called an ambulance.

Elmer recovering after the accident at his nephew's, Roy H. Buch, house. Photo courtesy of Marlene Buch.

The pulsating wail of an ambulance stopped Reuben Oberholtzer, who lived across the street, from his chores. He ran to the edge of the road and watched the ambulance speed out through the field towards Elmer. His younger brothers remember watching the same event from the Metzler One Room School House.

Elmer suffered a broken pelvis, 3 broken ribs, and internal bleeding. After being discharged from the hospital, he spent time recovering at the house of Roy Buch, who was his nephew. His leg healed nicely.[1]

Jacob M. Buch with his car in the 1920s. Photo courtesy of Marlene Buch.

A Tale of Two Bachelors

The story of the plantation continues when Daniel W. Buch deeded the farm to Elmer M. Buch on June 14, 1932.   Daniel continued to live on the farm until his death in 1945. At one point on April 20, 1944, he updated his will, stating "I give and bequeath all my livestock, farm equipment, furniture, household goods and personal effects to my two sons, Jacob Metzler Buch and Elmer Metzler Buch." This means much of what was on the aforementioned inventory list went to the two bachelor brothers. When Daniel passed, Jacob was 60 years old and Elmer was 54.

The men were not always planning on the bachelor life. And perhaps they were lookers. Elmer was 5 foot 4 and a half inches tall, with brown eyes and black hair, and a small mole on his forehead. He was a 150 pound man with a serious demeanor. Jacob weighted the same, though a half inch shorter than his brother.   His black hair framed his gray eyes.[2]

They had girlfriends, but little is known of them except for one. According to Arlene E. Hertzog, Elmer had planned on

197

marrying a Seigrist lady, who became pregnant. This apparently was more common than one might think. She died before the wedding could occur.

Jacob was the jollier of the two. At one point, Jacob bought a car. When giving a ride in the car, he would tell his passenger, "Hold onto your hat! We're going through Manheim!"

Sometimes Elmer went to Florida in the winter with an uncle, where he loved to go fishing. Allegedly, Elmer owned property in St. Petersburg, Florida, but my research into this has been

Jacob Metzler Buch with his nephew Arthur Franklin Buch. Photo courtesy of Marlene Buch.

Elmer (left) on one of his fishing trips to Florida.

inconclusive. He also loved raising watermelon and cantaloupe.

Overall the brothers were described as never really being in a rush and fairly easy going. Elmer would get a little excited now and then, but neither ever seemed to take farming that seriously. Perhaps this was because they had funds invested in Chase Manhattan, Caterpillar, and other

The plantation in the 1950s

companies. They would get checks in the mail all the time. They were financially secure because of this non-farming income.[3]

They would often loan out money to farmers in the area who were in need. At times, they were taken advantage of. They would loan out the money at no interest. In this, they tried to uphold the scripture which taught that "You shall not charge interest on loans to your brother, interest on money, interest on food, interest on anything that is lent for interest" (Deuteronomy 23:19-20 ESV). Farmers would eventually pay them back. A few of the farmers would then turn around and loan it out for interest, making money on the money the brothers had given them interest free. This obviously did not sit well with the brothers.

Through it all, the brothers remained honest and upright. They never gave anybody a bad deal. Clayton Oberholtzer would always talk about how honest and straight forward they were.[4]

The Housekeepers

From the 1930s, the time after their mother died, until the 1950s, the brothers had a housekeeper whose last name was Piket. But the housekeeper that most remember was Maddie Brubaker, who was born in 1900 in north-western Iowa. She was a part of the Stauffer-Pike Mennonite Church. She lived with the bachelors, in the northwest downstairs room of the house. Her room had the 1875 stove bought by Jacob S. Metzler. This stove is still with the family.

The 1875 coal stove bought by Jacob S. Metzler.

Maddie was in charge of the house. She told Jacob and Elmer what they were going to do around the house, and who was going to do what. And they accepted her recommendations. She was described as strict and bossy, but easy going. For example, she would tell them to change their clothes because it was wash day, and they would do it.[5] She passed away in the mid 1990s.

Memories of the Summer Kitchen

The house during their residence remained virtually unchanged. The addition built during the Jacob S. Metzler era continued to be used as a summer kitchen. Maddie carried on the tradition of moving the

1987: A picture of the south side of the house with the summer kitchen.

kitchen from the south-west corner of the main house to the summer kitchen in the spring and then back to main house in the fall. In the summers, she would do the cooking here, and she and the boys would eat out there as well. Sam Oberholtzer, who worked for the Buchs in the early sixties, can recall eating groundhog stew from a groundhog that Jacob shot in front of the house underneath the porch. While eating groundhog might seem a bit backwoods today, it was not an uncommon dish for the brothers. His brother Elmer was never much of a hunter.[6]

There was a cream colored kerosene cooking stove, that sat in the north eastern corner of the summer kitchen. The kitchen table sat in the north western corner. When they would eat at the table, it was typically just Maddie, Jacob, Elmer, and whatever hired hand was working with them at the time. There were times where they had more than one hired hand, but like Daniel Buch, this happened more during harvest times.

Inside the Plantation House

In the winter months, the main kitchen remained in the southwest corner of the stone house. One can still see where the stove pipe snaked up through the ceiling from the 6 plate stove that was in this kitchen. It was either a Majestic or a Pricer/Prizer. Elmer and Jake would often sit around this stove in the fall. Elmer would sit more hunched over. The kitchen table was in the north-west corner of the kitchen, where it was when I was a boy growing up, and where it still is today.

The parlor room from Daniel Buch's day remained a parlor into the 1960s until climbing the stairs became too difficult for Elmer to manage. The parlor eventually became Elmer's bedroom. It later contained a hospital bed in the early 1970s due to Elmer's failing health.

The northeast room was used as storage. Though with a corner cupboard and the bible closet one might think it would have been used as a sitting room, the brothers never entertained visitors much. When they did, it was in the kitchen or on the porch.

While the house may have remained unchanged, there were changes and modifications to the buildings on the farm itself.

The Block Butcher House

At the south-east corner of the house, Jacob and Elmer built a block butcher house in the 1945. I have speculated earlier that the Metzlers historically did their butchering here. I remember when my family bought the farm from the Elmer Metzler Buch estate, the butcher house still had butchering equipment in it such as a sausage maker.

The Wash/Coal House. We always referred to this as the butcher house.

Ironically, according to the hired hands who worked there in the 1950s and 1960s, this building was only ever used for coal storage and as a wash room. When I mentioned this to my grandmother, her comment was that these hired hands were much younger than she was. She, too, recalls it being a butcher house.

My mother always used this house as a garden shed; the only butchering we ever did here was during an avian flu outbreak that closed down all the area butcher shops in the early 1980s. We used the butcher house to slaughter our many chickens.

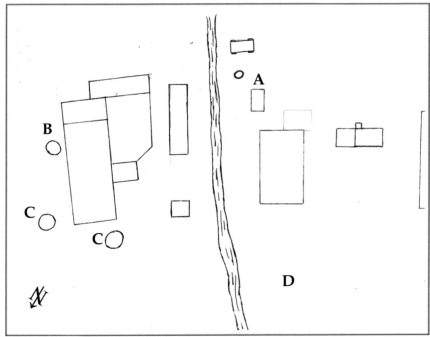

A. The butcher house is rebuilt as a block butcher house. B. The curved, 30-foot block silo is built. C. The round wire corncribs are built in the 1960s to provide more corn storage and drying areas. D. The log house no longer exists on the property.

Modifications to the Sweitzer Barn

In the early 1950s Elmer and Jacob added a block machinery shed to the southern end of the a barn and extending westward. They used the southern end of the pole barn to store machinery as well.

In 1954, the curved block silo was built. Clayton Oberholtzer helped Elmer and Jacob build the silo. He also taught them how to make silage. Silage is fermented, high-moisture stored fodder which can be fed to cattle and sheep. It is made from grass crops, including corn, sorghum or other cereals, using the entire green plant (including the grain) as well as hay crops for haylage. The brothers did not have the harvesting equipment themselves, so they had someone else come in a fill it. Sam Oberholtzer remembers Clayton battling silo gas the first few years. Silo gas is formed through the natural fermentation process of chopped forages shortly after they are placed in the silo. Nitrogen dioxide levels, the most common type of silo gas, reach a peak about three days after harvesting and can be deadly.

Somewhere in the 1930's to 1940s the brothers added onto the northern end of the barn with an extension that jutted out toward the northeast. There is some evidence that they hung tobacco in this section. Sam Oberholtzer recalls that by the time he worked on the farm, the Buch brothers stored their round bales there and housed some of their sheep underneath.

In the late 1960s, they added two round wire corn cribs. They do not appear in the 1950 and 1963 pictures. These round wire structure gave corn plenty of ways to dry. A wooden, slatted shaft dropped through the center, improving drying conditions.

Elmer and Jacob's Cars

Both had 1952 black Mainline or Customline Ford Sedans that they bought new the same year. Jacob had a two door Ford and Elmer had a four door Ford. Elmer parked his in the garage by the road and Jacob parked his in the garage at the end of the pole shed where the Carriage House Suites now stand.

Elmer's 1952 car

From Horses to Tractors

Though the house essentially did not change, there were many changes happening in farming. Lancaster County began a shift from horse farming to tractor farming in the 1940s.[7] By the

1960s, Elmer and Jacob had five different tractors, which was apparently not terribly uncommon.

They owned a John Deere H with an electric starter (it had the dual row cultivator attachment), an old hand crank John Deere A, a John Deere 50 (which they bought in 1952 and had the manure loader attachment), an Allis Chalmers G (which they bought in the middle 1950s), and an Allis Chalmers B (which was used, along with a small, single axel New Holland trailer, to pick up stones in the field). The G had an add-on manure spreader that was designed out west. It was operated by a Z belt.

In 1957, Elmer bought one of the first Allis Chalmers round bailers in the area; it made the small round bales. It was an Allis-Chalmers Roto-Baler. Sometimes, after a final cutting of hay, they would reportedly let bales set out in the field, just to show off to the neighbors.[8] They also owned a tobacco planter and plow. They had two discs. One was a little one that was just a typical disc. The other was a John Deere Killefer. This type of disc did not swivel in the middle. One would screw them apart to set them harder.

They had an old Ford Truck that Daniel Buch had bought. It was a straight body, had a two speed axel, and had 2 gears forward. In Jacob and Elmer's time, it was used to pick up stones and for clearing the fields.

Elmer was the primary farmer; Jacob worked as the treasurer for the D & E Telephone Company, a job he inherited from his father. Because of this, Elmer called the shots when it came to the farm. This included telling his hired hands how to do drive his tractors. Hired hands were trained in his way of driving and handling the tractors, which was the way he had learned to do it from his father. The equipment was always correctly maintained and treated with care.

For example, when hired hands drove the farm's John Deere 50, they were taught how to drive it, even if they already knew how to drive a tractor. This was known as the "Buch Way". They would be told how far to open the throttle, which was never

A John Deere A

A John Deere H

A John Deere 50

Allis Chalmers Roto Baler

An Allis Chalmers B

An Allis Chalmers G

Above Left: A photo from the 1950s showing Elmer's sheep.
Above Right: 1950s: Steers in the barnyard.
Right: Sheep by the house porch, resting in late morning shade. The wooden bench Jacob and Elmer often sat on can be seen on the porch. This bench is currently a part of the Hertzog Homestead Event Venue.
Below: Two picture of Elmer with his sheep. The photos above and below are courtesy of Marlene Buch.

more than two-thirds of the way. Of course, these instructions did not stop hired hands from opening the throttle up a bit more when they were out of sight of the house.[9]

Elmer rotated his crops, planting tobacco, hay, wheat, and corn in one field one year and then moving them to a different field. Wheat was stored in burlap bags on the barn floor, which were sold to the flour mill. Hay was in the northern and southern mows. Grain, after it was harvested in grain bin wagons, was at times just pulled into the barn and stored in these wagons. They also stored wheat and other grains in the granary.

Moments with Elmer and Jacob

The landscape of West Earl was much quieter then. There was no background noise from Route 222 that now lies a half mile away. Sound seemed to travel much further. Sylvan Horning, who lived a half mile away on West Metzler Road (and who was married to Anna Metzler, a second cousin to Jacob and Elmer), could hear Elmer singing to his chickens. Elmer kept chickens in the outbuilding behind the house.

In the evenings and the heat of the day, Elmer and Jacob would often sit on a wooden bench on the northern end of the porch. This bench came from their father and remained on the porch throughout the time my parents lived there until my wife and I moved onto the farm.

The Oberholtzer boys remember Elmer begging for candy. Maddie apparently would not allow him to have sweets due to

Daniel Buch's Ford truck with Alvin Martin

his health, but it did not stop him from trying.

He also apparently kept cheese in his car. Sam Oberholtzer remembers being called out to the car to sample it on occasion.

Jacob and Elmer raised sheep, so that they did not have to mow the lawn. At times they had upwards toward twenty plus sheep roaming around the front lawn, which they kept sheltered in a little outbuilding and also in the rolling shed. The sheep foraged for food the front yard, the backyard, and even behind the tobacco shed. When the sheep were behind the tobacco shed, they would nibble of the leaves of the tobacco that was hanging inside the ventilators slits in the tobacco shed. Tobacco acted as a natural wormer for them.

The End of the Buch Era

When Jacob died, he was at the Lancaster General Hospital recovering from a heart attack. Some time during the recovery period, he just keeled over. Jacob died January 20, 1966. His funeral was scheduled for Sunday, January 23rd, but a blanket of snow cancelled services until Monday.[10]

Soon after Jacob died, around 1970, Elmer decided to rent out the farm to his nephew, Roy H. Buch, and his son, Roy Buch Junior. By this time his ankles were swollen, and he could not move around very easily. He rented the farm to them from 1970 until 1976.

During this time, they raised hay, corn, wheat, and soybeans, and also raised fifty head of cattle in the barn. Elmer still lived in the main stone house, along with Maddie. Marlene, Roy Buch Junior's wife, can remember visiting Elmer in the kitchen, which was always hot, and remembers Maddie wearing dark glasses. Many times Maddie would provide Marlene with saffron.[6] When they would leave after visiting, Elmer would say "Someday I'll throw a stone in your garden." It was his way of saying "Go break a leg" or "Good luck."[11]

These pictures are from Elmer Metzler Buch's sale. Some of their household items as well as the layout and view of the yard and house can easily be seen. One can also see the wood fence that surrounded the year that kept the sheep from wandering.

She also remembers that on her wedding day, Elmer allowed Roy to "hide" his car, a Dodge Charger, in the garage near the road. Roy was a bit concerned about what some rascals might do to his car.[12]

Elmer died July 27, 1975 at the Ephrata Hospital. Elmer was all mixed up in the head, which sounds a lot like dementia.

How This Connects to the Hertzog Homestead

Elmer and Jacob Metzler Buch continued farming in the tradition of their forefathers. They modernized the farm through rebuilding the butcher house as a block structure and built the block silo behind the barn. Wire framed corn cribs were added during their time as well, a reflection on the increased corn production. The road that ran by the plantation was renamed Metzler Road in 1960.

\

The Elmer and Jacob Metzler Buch Family Tree

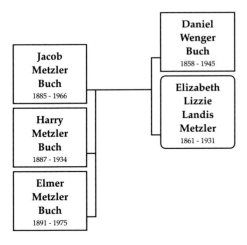

Harry Metzler Buch:
Of Reformers, Shootings,
and Shoes

The Buchs Threshing

Consumed By Fire

The 6:30 sun shone brightly in the western sky, beginning its descent toward the horizon. Harry Buch, his father Daniel, Milton Wanner, John Sauder, and others from the community were in the process of threshing an oat harvest, machinery whirring and clanging as dust filtered through the heavy, humid August evening. The threshing crew deftly worked the machine, owned by Milton Wanner, bagging the grain and baling the straw.

Grain stalks had been harvested earlier that day using a reaper - a piece of equipment with a large revolving wheel that drew the grain into knives which cut it off at the base. The oat stems were then bound using a binding machine and stacked onto flatbed wagons. After the wagons arrived at the barn and threshing had begun, Harry and Milton were on the wagon tossing the grain sheaves onto the threshing machine's conveyor belt. The belt skittered forward carrying the stalks toward the gaping maw of the machine. The machine separated the kernels from the stalks and discharged the grain through an auger into the bags Daniel was holding. When they were full, he would tie them off and then stack them along the wall of the threshing floor. The straw stalks moved on to a baler.[1]

Daniel rested his hand on the auger pipe as the bags below him filled and watched as the baler spit out long rectangular bales. The baler's rhythmic clang and rumble marked the end of another successful harvest. Harry yelled from the wagon and Daniel turned to catch sight of a spark falling from the baler onto the chaff and straw that littered the barn's threshing floor. Instantly it was ablaze. The fire spread quickly to every part of the big structure, and it was engulfed in flames by the time Akron and Ephrata fire companies arrived.

Harry's children, Arthur, Arlene, and Roy, were hustled to a car on Buch Road which ran in front of the farm, where they watched the scene unfold. Nothing could be done to save the barn. It was too far gone. Firemen decided, because the inferno of

Above: Harry Metzler Buch and Nora Miller Hackman's wedding photo. Below: A 1950's ariel photo of the Buch farm. Photo courtesy of Marlene Buch.

the barn and insufficient water, to focus their efforts on saving the house and adjoining buildings. Daniel and Harry managed to save all livestock that were quartered in the barn. No one was killed, but the loss of property must have seemed insurmountable.

Forty-five tons of straw, twenty-six acres of hay, and four acres of unthreshed oats were incinerated in the blaze. The threshing machine was in cinders. One thousand bushels of wheat and other crops, lost. Many farming implements that belonged to

Harry were gone. The barn, totally destroyed. The loss of the building, crops, and contents totaled $12,000 dollars, $162,500 in today's money.[2 3]

Harry M. Buch and Nora M. Hackman

This experience must have been hard for the Buch family. Let us back up a little. Harry Metzler Buch grew up on the Jacob Metzler Plantation; however, when he married Nora Miller Hackman, he never returned to live on the farm. Yet his family line and experiences are important because it is through them my father took over the farm from Harry's brothers who lived on the plantation.

Harry M. Buch

Harry married Nora Miller Hackman on October 29, 1912, at Nora's home. For their honeymoon, they traveled to Philadelphia, Atlantic City, and other points of interest. They took up residence at what was referred to as the Buch farm, along Buch Road. This road was also known as the "mud" road. It used to be that one could turn left out of the driveway of the Jacob Metzler Plantation, and make the first right on Buch Road, and Harry's farm was the first farm on the right. In the 1960's, the Route 222 highway came through splitting the farm and the road.

Descending from Martin Luther

Nora grew up in the Lincoln, PA, now a part of Ephrata. She was the daughter of Catherine (Katie) Bollinger Miller and Jacob Lane Hackman. What is interesting about Nora's mother's family line is that if you trace the Millers back, the line eventually

219

Above: A picture of when Harry and Nora were dating. Harry is pictured to the left and Nora is right beside him. Photo courtesy of Marlene Buch.

Below: Another picture of Harry and Nora dating. Harry is on the left with Nora down in front. Photo courtesy of Marlene Buch.

intersects with the Henkels. The Henkels eventually intersect with the Dentzers who intersect with the Wagners, where a certain Johann Georg Claes Wagner married a Anna Margaretha Luther who just happen to be the daughter of the reformer Martin Luther. Martin Luther and his wife, Katherine Von Bora were Nora's 12th great-grandparents (See Appendix I).[4, 5]

Martin Luther was born in November 10, 1483 and died on February 18, 1546. He was a German friar, a Catholic priest, professor of theology, and is generally credited with being the catalyst for the Protestant Reformation. He strongly protested the Roman Catholic Church's teaching that freedom from God's punishment for sin could be purchased for money. Most notably he confronted indulgence salesman Johann Tetzel, a Dominican friar, with his Ninety-Five Theses on October 31, 1517 when he nailed them to the door of All Saints Chruch. This eventually led to his excommunication by the Pope and condemnation as an outlaw by the Emperor.

Martin Luther

According to Luther, salvation was a gift through faith in Jesus Christ as a redeemer of sin, and not earned by good works. But this was not the only thing that irked the Catholic Church and the Pope. He believed that Bible was the only source of divinely revealed knowledge of God and that all baptized believers had direct access to God, being in themselves a royal priesthood. The Lutheran sect of Christianity would eventually bare his name.

He also believed in making Christianity accessible to all German speakers and published a translation of the Bible in the

German vernacular (instead of Latin). This had a tremendous impact on the reformation and German culture. This act in itself help foster the development of a standard version of the German language and even influenced the writing of an English translation, the Tyndale Bible. Luther eventually married Katharina von Bora. Other protestant priests soon followed in his footsteps.[6]

How this knowledge impacted Nora or whether she even knew about her heritage is difficult to tell. The family remained in Germany until the time of the Palatine exodus. Afterwards, they lived in and around the Ephrata area.

Harry and Nora's Family

In December of 1914, Harry and Nora both joined Metzler's Mennonite Church, where he was a treasurer for Sunday School and later a trustee after his father Daniel resigned.

They went on to have three children. Arthur F. Buch was born on November 10, 1913. His sister, Arlene Elizabeth Buch, was born on January 3, 1919. Roy Hackman Buch was born on July 31, 1920.

The Harry Buch family seemed to spend time with the Elmer Metzler Family. They attended a Snitz fest with the Metzlers on November 12th, 1931, where "they cut up 22 buckets of apples. Boiling the cider and apples the next day, all day and part of the night."[7] It yielded 58 crocks of apple butter. This seemed to be a yearly event for them.

Arlene recounts story of the time that her parents went to Canada with Elmer and Clara Metzler. She was eleven at the

Harry Buch threshing on the farm.
Photo courtesy of Marlene Buch.

222

Above: The Buch farm as it existed in 1913 before the barn burned in 1925 due to the fire sparked by the threshing machine. Photo courtesy of Marlene Buch. Left: Harry M. Buch posed in front of the barn. Below: Harry M. Buch in front of the barn with his horse. Photo courtesy of Marlene Buch.

From left to right: Arlene's school picture, Arthur at 9 months old, Roy Buch at 9 months old. Roy is one year old in the picture of him on the rocking horse. Below: Arlene, standing beside Arthur, pulling a wagon with Roy in it, just outside the barn before it burned.

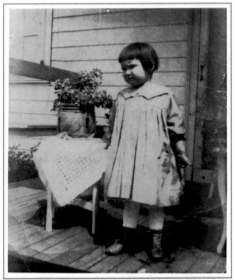

Arlene on the porch of the Buch Farm

Arlene, Roy, and Arthur.

time. Chester and Kate, friends of her parents, came and stayed with Arlene, Roy, and Arthur on the farm. It must have been mid-summer when this occurred. She tells how her and her brothers really wanted some ripe watermelon. Apparently there were watermelons near one of the cornfields. She and her brothers went out and cut off a bunch of watermelons. Unfortunately for them,

Roy Buch, age 14, on the farm.

Arthur and Roy shoveling snow.

225

they were not ripe yet. Mom and dad were NOT happy when they came home.

My grandmother also tells the story about how she went to Elmer Metzler's to visit with her cousins. It had just snowed and they wanted to go on a sleigh ride. There was no sleigh available, but they were not deterred. They hitched up "Boy" the Mule to Elmer's manure sled and rode that around the snowy land. I am sure it was quite a site for the neighbors.

My grandmother and her brother Roy went along with Elmer Metzler and his four oldest children to the Harrisburg Farm Show. They repeated this visit multiple years in the thirties.

On August 27, 1940, Arlene traveled with Elmer and Clara to the World's Fair in New York City, leaving at 5 in the morning. Due to a faulty water hose in Elmer's car, they did not arrive at the fairgrounds until 10:30 AM. They returned home on August 29th.[8]

Who Owned the Buch Farm?

This farm was owned by the Buchs, though not initially by Harry. A newspaper reports that on August 7, 1925, when the aforementioned fire destroyed a large bank barn, wheat crop, and threshing rig, the barn belonged to Daniel W. Buch, Harry's father-in-law.

In 1930 Harry began to develop kidney trouble, but as time passed, he seemed to be improving. On April 8, 1931, Daniel W. Buch sold the farm to Harry and Nora for $13,205.00, about $206,000 in today's money. Then in 1932, something happened that would alter the family landscape.

Harry Is Shot

The October 1932 morning was brisk as Harry and his cousin picked their way over corn stubble toward the Buch house. Guns were cradled in the crooks of their arms; they had been out

One of the last pictures of Harry and Nora before he died.

Nora and Harry

hunting rabbits and pheasants. No word on what the take was that day. As they neared the house, his cousin's gun accidentally discharged, leaving Harry's foot badly mangled. It caused Harry a long time of suffering. The story as I initially understood it was that he eventually died as a result of this injury, but my grandmother says this was not the case.

About a week before his death, he had a nervous stroke and was taken to the Lancaster General Hospital. Arlene, his daughter, donated a pint of blood to him. He died at 12:15 from complications on Wednesday on January 24, 1934, at 46 years of age. Harry's second cousin, Elmer Metzler, and his wife Clara helped Nora arrange the funeral while neighbors pitched in with the farm chores.[9]

The January 28th funeral was the largest ever at Metzler's Mennonite Chruch. Brother Benjamin Wenger and Bishop John Sauder preached using the text Matthew 24:44. It reads "Therefore be ye also ready: for in such an hour as ye think not the Son of man cometh." There was also preaching in the overflow section in the basement of the church by Bishop Noah Landis and Brother John W. Hess.[10]

Life After Harry

Arlene was 15 when her father died. She and her two brothers continued to live on the farm with Nora. Soon after, Arthur married Mary Auker, and they moved into the retirement house that Jacob S. Metzler's twin John built, now owned by Elmer Metzler. They were living here in 1937. The journals of Elmer Metzler note that their "household needed supervising, he and Mary have limited mentality."[11] Roy was married in February 8, 1941. During this

Wayne and Nora Brubaker

time she, her mother and her brothers visited the Elmer Metzler's farm (twin John Metzler's farm) often.

Nora married Wayne Brubaker, on January 2, 1937. Wayne was born on January 13, 1878. He was one of the six people who founded the Miller, Hess and Company Shoe factory in Akron.

The Miller, Hess and Company Shoe Factory

The factory organized on April 17, 1900 to manufacture shoes and boots. Initially, there were four founding partners: Peter B. Miller, Albert N. Wolf, Simon P. Hess (a brother-in-law to Albert), and Frank J. Conlin. By the end of December, three more partners joined in the venture: Wayne E. Brubaker (my step-great grandftaher), Charles M. Conlin, and Samuel N. Wolf, a brother to Albert. Frank J. Conlin left the company in 1902.[12]

Top: Arlene Buch on the John S. Metzler Farm. She was a server at a wedding that was held there, most likely a Metzler wedding.
Below: Arlene Buch and Fred Hertzog on a double date with David Burkholder and Edna Gehman. Arlene and Fred are in the back. David Burkholder's father founded the Green Dragon Farmer's Market where Arlene first met Fred.

Wayne and Nora's home on the corner of Main & State Street in Akron, PA. The Miller, Hess and Company Shoe Factory can be seen in the background.

The Conlins were the cobblers of the group, having learned their trade from their immigrant father who brought the skill from Ireland. Once the partners learned to make shoes, they sold their shares of the company and discontinued the partnership.[13]

Operations began in Elias Wolf's warehouse, on the third floor, along Front Street across from the Akron depot. They made

Highland Shoe Company, a division of The Miller-Hess Shoe Company in 1934.

100 pairs of shoes each day for the first two years. Then, they bought a new two story brick building at the corner of Main and seventh street, officially purchasing in in 1911 for $6,000. This allowed them to produce over 500 pairs of shoes daily. That year the company incorporated with S.N. Wolf as president, Wayne Brubaker as Vice president, and Al Wolf as Secretary and treasurer.
14

The Move to Akron

Roy and his new bride Viola Esbenshade took over the Buch farm, and Wayne, Nora, and Arlene moved to the corner of Main and State Street in Akron, PA. The house is still there today. Apparently, between the years that Nora was married and Roy Buch became married, Arlene, Arthur, and Roy would keep house at the farm at times while Nora and Wayne lived in the house at Akron.

Arlene, now around 21, worked at the Miller-Hess Shoe Company, a job she most likely acquired because of her step-father. She remembers boxing shoes and even working with the stitching. She worked there four years.

Oberholtzer's General Store

While living in Akron, the main source of goods came from Oberholtzer's General Store, located across from what is now Weiser's Grocery Store, on the corner of Ninth and Main Streets. Arlene used to walk there to get groceries for Wayne, her mother, and herself. At time, she also would pick up groceries for her brother Arthur and his wife Mary, who apparently were not the

Arthur and Mary Buch with their children: Dorthy, Eugene, and Carl.

best at managing money. She would lug them down the road a little over a half mile to the house he lived in just outside of Diamond Station. There was not much of a walk there, being that it was mostly overgrown with shrubbery. Arthur was often describe as "being the way he was" or "not being all there." They had three children, Carl, Eugene, and Dorothy. Dorothy lived with Wayne and Nora because of the situation at Arthur's.

Ironically, Arthur did go on to help co-found the Diamond Springs water company in Akron, where he worked until his death. While at times he causes issues at work, the owner always made sure he had a place to work as long as he lived.

In her twenties, Arlene spent much time on neighboring farms. Specifically, she was close to Ruth Metzler, her 3rd cousin, who grew up on the John S. Metzler farm. She was also close to Edna Gehman, who eventually married David Burkholder. Fred and Arlene went on many double dates with this couple. She also seems to have enjoyed hiking and at least one time visited Ocean City, MD.

Arlene Buch and Edna Gehman at Ocean City, MD

Arlene Elizabeth Buch Marries Fredrick Hertzog

Arlene met Fred Hertzog at the Green Dragon Farmer's Market. She was most likely with Rose Gheman who was dating Davie Burkholder. Davie was the son of the son of the owner of Green Dragon. On March 17, 1945 Arlene married Fred F. Hertzog, the son of Stephen Hertzog and Sallie Frederick of Lincoln. In the tradition of prior generations, they were married at the bride's house, in Akron at the house of Wayne and Nora. It was Saint Patrick's Day and, according Fred's sister, Esther White, a dusting of snow covered the yard. After they married, they resided on

Arlene Buch and Fred Hertzog wedding photo

a farm just north of the Diamond Station intersection of North Farmersville Road on a farm to the right. My father, whose story is told in the next chapter, was born on this farm.

The Tractor Disaster at Diamond Station

While Fred and Arlene were living on the Diamond Station Farm, they continued the tradition of helping their neighbors. One neighbor borrowed Fred's tractor for reasons now unclear. What is clear is that, although he might have known how to drive a tractor, he did not know how to drive Fred's tractor. When he went to back it out of the barn, the tractor lurched forward

Fred's tractor hanging through the front of the Diamond Station Farm.

through the front of the barn, over the forebay, and fell toward the barnyard floor. The rear tire caught on the barn floor causing it to hang at a crazy angle.

Surprisingly, no one was seriously hurt. And the farmers were able to hoist the tractor down virtually undamaged.

On May 25, 1948, Arlene and Fred moved off the Diamond Station farm onto the farm in Lincoln. The 31 acre farm, originally belonging to Mary Wenger, was bought for $27,750 dollars, about $272,800 in today's money.

How This Connects to the Hertzog Homestead

Harry Metzler Buch grew up on the plantation. While he moved off the plantation and onto what has become known as the Buch farm, he most likely helped his father out at times on the farm. My family line comes through this line of Buchs and Metzlers.

The Harry Metzler Buch Family Tree

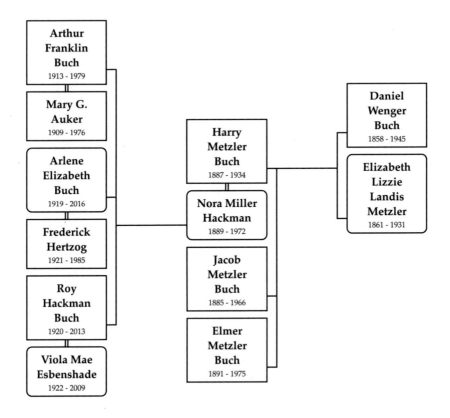

K. Scott Hertzog

Kenneth Buch Hertzog:
The End of a Farming Legacy

Photograph by Lynette Sauder

An Inadequate Capture

Capturing the stories of my father and mother's place in this history reminds me of the time my wife Kristen and I visited Switzerland and stood at the edge of a cliff looking down into a valley overshadowed by Jungfrau. This mountain peak of the Swiss Alps is breathtaking. I tried to capture this scene in photographs as can be seen below, but despite the limited beauty one can see, it inadequately captures the moment, the experience of being there, and feeling the bite of the chilled Swiss air. I was five years old when my father and my mother moved onto Jacob Metzler's planation. Much of my family's role and interaction on the farm comes through the memories of growing up there. And though perhaps incomplete, I will paint the best picture I can.

The Jungfrau Mountain peak in the Switzerland when Kristen Hertzog and I visited my ancestral homeland.

Born on the Mountain Springs Resort

Kenneth Hertzog at 3 years old.

I feel a vacancy when it comes to my father's early life. There are so many stories that I do not know, and that, since he passed away in 2012, I cannot ask. My father did not talk much about his growing up years.

My mother and father were stoic people, of solid Mennonite Germanic stock, born and raised in Lancaster County, Pennsylvania. They were reserved with outsiders, as with the immediate family, but at the same time held a fascination with other cultures as evidenced in their hosting of international students from China and Japan over Christmas time.

Kenneth Buch Hertzog was born on January 30th, 1946 at the old Ephrata Hospital. This was originally the Mountain Springs Hotel, once a vacation destination where guests could be revitalized in the

Fred Hertzog standing beside his Chevy Stytlemaster.

waters that flowed there. Abraham Lincoln once slept in its rooms. My grandmother remembers my grandfather driving her to the hospital in their Chevy Stylemaster. Since there were no elevators in the hospital, she was forced to climb the stairs to the second floor while in labor. His sister, Nancy, was born on October 22, 1950 in the new Ephrata Hospital on Martin Avenue.

As a young boy, Kenneth helped out around the farm. On any given Saturday, he and Fred could be found sitting at local

Kenneth at 5 years old.

auctions as the auctioneer prattled on. Dad loved that atmosphere, and it connected him to the people in the community. This love of sales went with him throughout his life, perhaps at times much to my mother's chagrin. Certainly to my grandmother's. After my grandfather passed away, it took Leon Hurst, Nancy Hertzog's husband, and my father two days to remove all the "treasures" he had accumulated from sales.

My father attended Ephrata Public High School where he served as an officer in the Future Business Leaders of America. A year after he graduated in 1963, he and some of his buddies decided to attend the 1964 World's Fair in New York City. They took a pickup truck, placed a camper on the bed, and went on their trip. My brother, Doug, remembers him telling how they smoked cigars in the back of the truck on the way to New York.

He had a love for music. His record collection contained everything from Johnny Cash to the Beach Boys and the Beatles.

Ken with his guitar in the farmhouse on Meadow Valley Road.

This love spawned a rudimentary ability to play guitar and banjo. Growing up, I only remember him loving bluegrass and county gospel. I remember going with him to see the Lewis Family, a country gospel group, at the Guernsey Barn on Route 30.

Most of his life, my father worked for the Horst Group in the excavation division. He started out with A & C Excavating. This later evolved into Bilran Excavating, and still later became known as Horst Excavating. He was a hard worker, rising at 4 in the morning to go to work and arriving back home at around 5 in the afternoon.

Prior to this, he worked in a few other jobs. One story tells how he was working at Grants in Ephrata. After Christmas, the owners threw out an artificial Christmas tree which had a few twisted branches. He rescued it from the dumpster, and this became our tree for most of our growing up years.

He worked for short time at Carter Sewing. My mom once said that "you never saw a more miserable man during time he worked there." I do not think he worked there very long, perhaps only a few weeks. He also worked at his step-grandfather's shoe factory in Akron for a time, in the Highland Shoe Company, a division of the Miller Hess Shoe Company.

Growing up, he, like his ancestors, attended Metzler's Mennonite Church. When the Vietnam War broke out, he, as many of his friends did, registered as a Conscientious Objector. The United States government provided alternative service for Conscientious Objectors who were drafted. My father was drafted into 1W Service (At Work Conscientious Objectors) in Morristown, New Jersey, sometime in 1967. He worked at Morristown Memorial Hospital as a

Ken in front of his apartment in Morristown, NJ during 1W Service.

janitor. He lived in an apartment with John Nolt, Mahlon Zimmerman, and Glenn Eberly.

My grandmother and my mother remember a time when my father accidentally shot the family dog. Fred and Arlene had a black dog named Rex that the family adored. One day, when my mother was visiting my father, he went out to shoot rats from underneath the corncrib. When he saw a rat, he leaned down, aimed, and then fired his 22. At that moment, Rex saw the rat and dashed toward it. The dog was the one who ended up dead. Nancy, dad's sister, was furious at him for killing their dog. He apparently was pretty upset himself.

He lived life in the fast lane, literally. He had a passion for cars. He owned one or two Corvairs and blew the engine out of one. On Sundays, Maple Raceway used to open up their track as a safer place for people to race their cars. He took part in this, and must have won a few times. I remember seeing trophies from these days perched on shelves around his shop. But as a slew of speeding tickets at some pretty high speeds can attest, he did not keep his speed to the raceway.

Above: Dad's 1968 GTO he bought for $4000. He eventually sold it for $20,000
Below: Ken with his purple Corvair.

He owned a motorcycle, though not for very long. One time, he was traveling down 772 from Rothville toward Schaum's Corner, where it crossed 272. There is a bend in the road before it travels over a bridge that crosses the Cocalico Creek. On this bend he apparently hit gravel. The cycle spun out from under him, scraping up his leg but not seriously injuring him. Still, my grandmother made him get rid of the cycle. This happened before he met my mother.

In 1968, he bought a brand new GTO for $4,000.00. In 2005, he sold it on Ebay to a buyer in Qatar for $20,000. The vehicle was used as one of our main cars up into the 1980s. When I married Kristen Anselmo in 1996, we used the GTO to carry us from Metzler's Mennonite Church to Willow Valley Resort in Willow Street, PA for our wedding reception.

Arlene Stauffer Hess

My mother, Arlene Stauffer Hess, was born on May 20, 1946. She was the fourth daughter of Miles Stoner Hess and Lottie Witmer Stauffer. She, like Maria Metzler, was a descendent of the martyr Hans Hess, whose story is told earlier in this book. Her mother died when she was only six from a tumor in her throat, leaving Miles to take care of her and her brother Leon Hess, who at the time was only two. Her other siblings were married by this time. This pushed her into

From Left: Ruth Stauffer Cramer, Lottie Stauffer Hess. and Margie Longenecker Hess

maternal responsibilities quite early.

My mother loved school. She loved Shakespeare, musicals, and poetry. She loved learning and studying, and iceskating on her father's pond. Her father, since he had not attended school past the eighth grade, did not see the value in education. So when she finished her eighth grade school year at Bergstrausse School, it was unfortunately her last. She did eventually go on to obtain her General Equivalency Diploma. At the age of 19, she moved out and went to live with her sister Verna and her husband, Harold Zimmerman, in Ephrata, PA.

She was a diligent and precise bookkeeper. While she was still at home, she kept the books for her father's egg business. When Lloyd Snader, who married her oldest sister Irene, bought the business from Miles, she keep books for him as well. After she went to live with her sister Verna, she kept books for Harold Zimmerman, who was a farmer and an inventor. She worked as a secretary for the Horst Group in the late 1960s when its head offices were still in New Holland. She eventually helped my father acquire a job there.

Kenneth Marries Arlene

When my mother and father became engaged, they did not exchange rings like most do today. Jewelry as such was not looked highly upon in the Mennonite Church. Instead, my father bought my mother a GE Stereo with a record player. This sat in my parents' living room in the Jacob Metzler Plantation for years. I listened to many of my father's sixties rock albums and mother's musicals on it.

My parents were married at Hinkletown Mennonite Church on March 1st, 1969. Glenn Eshleman, who was the founder of Sight and Sound Theaters in Strasburg, was the photographer for their wedding. They went to Florida for their honeymoon.

Above: Ken and Arlene in front of their engagement gift - a GE Stereo.
Below: Arlene and Ken in front of Ken's childhood home.

Kenneth and Arlene Hertzog Wedding photo taken outside of Hinkletown Mennonite Church by Glenn Eshleman. March 1, 1969.

My father loved both hunting and fishing. The summer after my mother and father were married, they took some trips to the Susquehanna where my father would row out to a sand bar. My mother would sit in the boat reading a novel while my father fished.

Kenneth Scott Hertzog's Early Life

I was born on December 30, 1970 at the Ephrata Hospital. I only have a few recollections about living at 230 South Market Street. Some I remember; some I was told. Apparently, when I was able to crawl, my father was working down in the basement of the house and had left the basement door open. I, perhaps being a bit curious, crawled my way over to the steps, and tumbled down. I do not remember if my mother saw it happen,

My father fishing on the Susquehanna

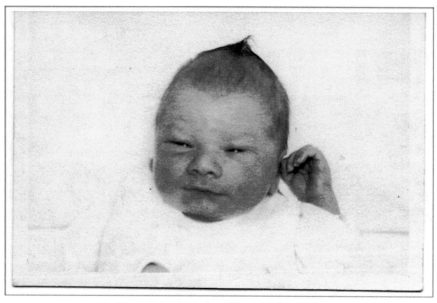

Kenneth Scott Hertzog December 30, 1970

but I am told that my father caught me as I tumbled off the last step toward the concrete floor below.

I am told how I stuck a metal kitchen knife in between the top of the range of the stove and the oven portion. I apparently got quite the shock. My mother had the knife for years afterwards. Apparently, when I was one or two, I tossed my blocks through the front window of the house. This was a preamble to the many other windows I would break later in life when I was much older and should have known better.

At one point before we moved down to Jacob Metzler's Plantation, my father was in the barn feeding cattle. There must have been quite a bit of hay lying on the ground. It was not unusual for us to walk around the farm barefoot; this must of been the case for my father as well. Hidden in the was a pitchfork with its tines upturned. He stepped down on one of the tines sending it straight through his foot. His toes never looked quite the same after this incident.

Fred and Arlene Hertzog's farm on 230 South Market Street where my father grew up and I spent the first six years on my life. Photo courtesy of Leann Hurst.

Douglas Kent Hertzog, my brother, was the last of my siblings to be born while my family lived on this farm. He was born on January 11, 1973.

My Family Moves to
the Jacob Metzler Plantation

In 1976, more than 200 years after the first structure was erected on the property, Kenneth Buch Hertzog, 7 generations removed from Jacob N. Metzler, bought the farmstead at an estate sale with the help of his father, Fred Hertzog.

He moved his family, his wife Arlene and his sons, Scott and Doug, from the farm on which he had grown up outside of Lincoln to the Jacob Metzler Plantation. Later that year, they adopted a Korean girl, Jessica Kim, who was born March 15, 1974, and two years later, Jason Daniel, born on November 7, 1978, completed the family.

My father continued to work at Horst Group as well as farm the 48 acres his ancestors had cultivated. Working two jobs left him exhausted much of the time. He raised anywhere from 40 to 50 head of cattle. Some of these dad bought; others were bought by Fred, and dropped off much to my father's chagrin.

The Dump Truck Fiasco

It was an early 1980s spring day. My father at this point was a foreman for Horst and one of his responsibilities was to make sure equipment made it from one job to the other. On one particular day, one of the dump truck left a Horst employee stranded on 322 as it runs up over Cornwall Mountain. My dad, being a foreman, went out to see what he could do.

The truck turned over but would not start. He took a can of gas from the back of his truck, and then took the air filter off the dump truck. He told the man behind the wheel of the dump truck to try starting it again after he had poured gasoline in the carburetor. The man did not wait.

As my father poured some gas into the carburetor, the man turned the key in the ignition. The engine spouted flames and roared to life. My father's clothing instantly caught fire. He fell to ground engulfed in flames. The man behind the wheel heard him yell and got out of the truck. He rolled him to put out the flames.

An ambulance took him to Ephrata Hospital where remained for over two weeks. He had third degree burns on his arms and some on his face as well. During this time, my siblings and I were shuttled between my Grandma Hertzog's house and my mom's sisters' places. My father was in the Intensive Care Unit, so it was a week before we as children could see him.

I probably did not realize how serious the whole situation was, nor the strain it put on my mother. I was excited to watch TV

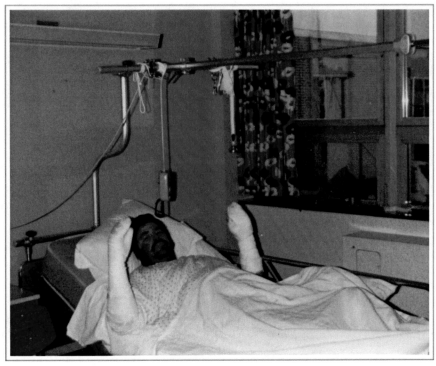

Ken Hertzog in the Ephrata Hospital after the accident.

shows after school, since we had no TV at home. I loved *Green Acres* and *Mr. Ed*.

The one thing this incident showed me was the generosity of family and how they stick by in thick and thin. My mother remembers both church and family giving time and financially.

Because they had to graft skin from my father's legs to cover his hands, it took years before his fingers and knuckles toughened up. I remember how they easily were chapped in the winter and how easily they would split open.

The Sixty Foot Tower

Initially silage was shoveled down out of the block silo that still stands behind the barn. I still remember dad locking the wooden, numbered silo doors into place. In the late 1970's, Dad

The original block silo that Jacob and Elmer Metzler Buch built. My father used this silo the first years on the farm.

had a 60 foot stave silo built, complete with a silo unloader and bunk feeder that stretched across the current barnyard. I can still remember the shuttle work its way up and down the conveyer belt as silage was delivered to steers, who would step up on a concrete step to reach the beige tiled trough. This silo is visible on arial photos from that time period.

One time my second cousins, Melody and Lottie Herr, daughters of John and Esther Herr, were visiting. At ten O'clock in the morning, we were outside playing. A row of concrete cement blocks were stacked against the lower staves of the silo. The staves were notched together and held with metal cabled rods that ringed the silo a foot apart from each other for the first 15 feet and then increasingly spaced apart. My brothers and I would prove bravado by scaling these rings. We never went extremely high, but as a nine-year-old, it felt like conquering the world.

That morning, I decided I was going to impress Melody and Lottie by showing them how high I

The number 15 silo door.

could climb. I began to scamper up the rings. I was about 15 feet up, looking down at my cousins as I climbed, proud of how high I was, when I ran straight into a wasp nest.

I knew that wasps often built nests on the silo. My father often knocked them down, perhaps one of the most memorable being a hornets nest he took down from the block silo behind the barn. I do not know why I did not look up that day.

I let go and plummeted to ground, landing right on top of the cement blocks. I do not remember how I ended up in the house, but I do remember lying on the patterned linoleum kitchen floor near the basement door, bruised and in pain from the multiple wasp stings I sustained. My mother had placed a damp cloth on my forehead. My pride was bruised as well. Luckily, no bones were broken.

One summer when I was around 20 years old, I climbed the same stave silo rings onto the metal roof of adjacent the machine shop. My dad must have asked me to pitch the roof because I lugged the pitch bucket, brush, and squeegee up the silo and was diligently working the tar across the slope of the roof. I had turned the radio dial to the Christian Radio Station FM 90.3 WJTL, something I often did while working around the barn.

On this particular day, WJTL was running a contest where the seventh caller after certain song would win a Creation prize pack along with a chance to win tickets to the Creation Festival held in Mount Union, PA. I was determined to win. There was one problem.

This was the days before cellphones. In order for me to be the seventh caller, I had to climb back down the silo rungs, sprint across the barnyard, scale the barnyard fence, and then enter the front feed entry to pick up the phone and then dial the station. I was not deterred.

I pulled back on the squeegee, spreading the thick metallic liquid across tin roof. The song came on and I dropped the squeegee. Darting to the edge of the roof, I grabbed for the silo rings...and missed. Inertia propelled me over the edge, and I fell

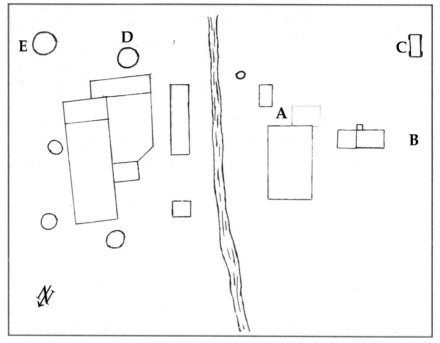

A. Side porch is converted into a sun room. B. The tobacco shed blew down in the 1960s, and was used as trash storage up until the 1980s. C. The rolling machine shed was moved and used to raise chickens. D. A 60-foot stave silo was built complete with a silo unloader and a bunk feeder that jutted out into the barnyard. This silo was torn down in the early 1990s. E. A grain bin was built better handle grain storage, effectively making the granary in the barn obsolete. It, too, was torn down in the 1990s.

hard onto the silo unloader crank right below me. I saw stars. My leg was in pain. I did not make it to the phone.

The stave silo was torn down in the early 1990s when my father decided not to farm and sold it. As the years had passed, it became increasingly harder to make money farming while working a second job. The bunk feeder was also torn out at this time.

Cattle on the Homestead

But before all this, I can remember running around the barnyard barefoot because after all manure would always wash off. Occasionally dad would get steers that were so tame that we would herd them near the concrete barnyard wall and climb on them, riding them around.

Riding cattle was not an anomaly for us. My father and mother helped us raise and show steers for 4-H at the age of 8. Because we worked so closely with these animals, they would become really tame. I can still remember riding on the back of Herman and George, especially George. These were my very first Hereford steers.

Stalls were cleaned out partially by hand, but mostly we used a small skid loader that actually was able to fit in the narrow doorways of the stalls. Manure was loaded onto a New Holland manure spreader, and then spread on the fields.

Don't Throw Rocks at Glass Windows

Chickens were raised for eggs and meat in the little outbuilding behind the house, the same building where Daniel

Scott with a steer at the New Holland Stockyards, most likely the New Holland Fair.

Buch and Jacob and Elmer raised chickens. In the following years, the chickens were moved to the rolling machine shed. There is evidence as well that the southern end of the barn also housed chickens. I remember there being roosts of some sort there.

This southern end had a bank of single paned glass windows. During the first months of us moving onto the farm, I somehow thought it would be a great idea to throw rocks at these panes. I honestly to this date do not know what I was thinking. There was a thrill to launching each rock towards the glass, and then hearing the glass shatter on to the concrete floor behind. Pane after pane fell to my targeted aims.

And then mother rounded the corner.

I can still remember running away from her through the meadow that used to sit behind the barn toward the cemetery. I am not sure where I thought I was going. Her stalking form came after me; she was furious and rightly so.

The rolling machine shed housed the chickens in later years and sat near the western end of the solar array close to where the lime kiln was. The chickens raised here were solely for meat, and many times tied into 4-H projects my brothers were involved with. Mostly capons, I believe.

Besides the chickens and cattle, we had other animals as well, but only really as 4-H projects. We initially joined 4-H raising rabbits. Later we raised pigs and even sheep. I even had a Holstein heifer, named Mary Jo, that I showed at the PA Farm Show and local fairs for FFA.

FFA was an important part of my life. I was a member of the Eastern Lancaster County FFA Chapter at Garden Spot High School. This organization taught much about wood working, engines, judging cattle, and working the soil. I earned my Green Hand, Red Rose, and Keystone Degrees and earned awards in daily and land judging. My senior year I served the Chapter's Vice-President.

Above: Scott with his FFA Heifer Mary Jo. Below: Scott riding Herman, his first Hereford 4-H steer, with Doug and George, his other 4-H Hereford steer in the background.

Above: The Eastern Lancaster County FFA Chapter in 1989. I am seated behind our advisor Cliff Day. Below Left: I am about to receive my Keystone Degree at the Pennsylvania Farm Show. Blow Right: In 2016, I wore my FFA jacket for an FFA event at Penn Manor High School where I teach. It was in support of National FFA week and an organization that is still dear to my heart.

The Jacob Metzler Plantation in 1987.

The Crop Painted Tapestry

My father raised a variety of crops. Corn was obviously a staple, raised to feed the cattle, turned into ground feed and silage. Hay was also important. He also raised rye, soybeans, and tobacco at various times.

I have many memories of working the field with my dad. He would hook his John Deere 2510, which he bought used in 1970, to a four bottom plow to turn over the ground. After plowing the fields, he would then switch to his Allis Chalmers disc with a wooden drag.

I remember riding the drag with my brother Doug. We found this extremely exhilarating. At one point we thought it would be fun to throw ourselves off the front of the drag into the soft loam, allowing the drag to push us into the ground. I have no idea who came up with this idea or whether it might have first happened as an accident, but I do remember it happening multiple times. My father never stopped it as far as I can recall.

261

I remember the first time my father allowed me disc the freshly plowed fields. Though I was only eight, I had driven the tractor before and knew how to raise and lower the hydraulic system connected to the disc. I still remember lowering the disc onto the field where the cropland butted up against the pasture behind the barn. When I reached the other end of the field, I turned the tractor around, the wheels grabbing the grass of the waterway, lining me up for my next pass over the field. It was at the other end of the field, near the pasture behind the barn, where I ran into trouble.

When I turned the wheels to line up the tractor for the next pass over the field, nothing happened. The 2510 just lunged forward toward the pasture fence. I frantically twisted the steering wheel. The tractor slammed into the log fence post, the front kicked up, and then the engine sputtered to a stop. My heart was pounding.

Tractors have two brakes: one stopping the right tire allowing the tractor to rotate sharply right and one completing the same action to the left. Both brakes pushed at the same time stop the tractor. My father had never told me this, though in retrospect, this was not hardly surprising. Mom tells the story of a time soon after they were married. My father asked her to drive a tractor home from a field they were renting to the farm on Market Street. He never told her how to shift gears, so she drove the tractor home in first gear. It took her forever.

The reality was that, though we were young with my brother Doug and I being only 6 and 8, it was a necessity for us to help around the farm.

Another time when I was seven, I remember driving the tractor in the freshly harvested cornfield on an early October day. The husks and stalks had been raked into rows with a circular tractor rake. Dad had placed me on the tractor in first gear, showed me how to line up the baler with the row. As the baler worked its way up the row, the tines scooped the fodder into the maw of the baler and compressed it into the baler chute. While some New Holland balers had a mechanism that kicked the 3 foot, 70 pound bales out onto the flat wagon that was hitched to the baler, our's required one person, typically my father, to pull the bales off the baler, then turn, and hand off the bale to a second person, typically mother, who stacked it on an 8 tiered stack. That October must have been particularly dry because I can remember dust being kicked up everywhere as I looked back over my shoulder at my parents laboring on the wagon behind me.

When the wagon was filled, it was pulled onto one of the threshing floors, and bales were stacked into one of the side mows. My father stored hay, straw, and fodder bales in these mows. At times my brother and I would make straw tunnels through mows which made for some dusty fun. At other times we would climb the rafters overhead, playing brumsock.

Brumsock is basically the game of tag. A burlap feedbag is tied into a knot. One person, the one who is "it", stands on the ground with the knotted bag in hand. The rest scramble throughout the barn, up into the rafter and around the tobacco rails, trying to get out of reach and to dodge any bags tossed his way.

There were three hay holes in the floor that were used to deliver the straw, hay, and fodder to the steers in the pens below. The most northern and southern hay holes dropped into stalls. The middle one was used exclusively for hay, since that one led down to the second feed entry in the barn, where food for the cattle was stored. I can remember a few times where, as I was tossing a bale of hay down into the feed entry or a bale of straw into the stable, I lost my balance and went tumbling in. Thankfully there was always hay below or straw to break my fall.

As kids, we used to love riding the back of the corn planter or the back of the grain drill as dad went back and forth seeding the field. My father always seemed at peace as he drove his tractors over the fields.

Curiosity takes a Finger

One year, my father was pulling the weathered, green grain drill up the hill, away from our house. A grain drill is a machine that is pulled behind a tractor and planted grain. Jason, who was seven at the time, rode on the back stepping board. I was in the house, probably thinking I was too old to do such childish things. The gears whirred and clicked as grains dropped from the hopper into the ground. My brother watched this with curiosity. That curiosity ended horrifically.

A sharp cry from my brother caused my father to jam and lock the brakes on the John Deere. This stopped the gears of the grain drill as well, since it was wheel driven. When he came to my brother, he saw Jason's index finger jammed into the gears of the grain drill. If it had been power driven by a PTO shaft, as many farm implements are, it would have been a bigger disaster, perhaps even fatal. The PTO, the Power Take Off, powers farm implements via the tractor's engine. My father backed up the machine to get his finger free.

Later, the finger was describe as being like hamburger. There was no way to salvage it. There was some minor damage to some of the other fingers as well. After some time at the Ephrata Hospital, he came home.

Jason never let the loss of his finger stop him from making the most of his life. He was an accomplished trumpeter through out high school, and is a master at coding computer programs.

Harvesting Corn

My father harvested corn using the two row, New Idea corn picker he borrowed from his father, Fred. He may have eventually owned it. I do not remember. In fact, I do not remember him selling off much of the farm equipment when he and mom made the decision to stop of farming. This may have happened when I attended college at Hesston College in Hesston, Kansas.

I have fond memories of climbing up the thin metal rungs of the red bin wagon and clinging to the sides as my father made pass after pass down the corn rows and the long neck of the corn picker flung ears into the wagon's maw. After the corn filled the wagon half way, it was easier for us to find footing on the ears. Though it was easy to avoid the flinging ears of corn, we sometimes got hit when my father turned at the end of the row. And then there were the times my brothers and I pelted each other with them.

Corn was stored in the wire rimmed corn cribs, with a wooden slatted center piece that allowed the corn to dry. Corn was dumped into the crib via an elevator. Dad lined up the chute of the bin wagon to the elevator, he would spin the door open and allow the corn to spill into the elevator.

Later in the year, Sensenig's portable hammer hill would come out and grind the corn into feed. Once the corn was ground up and inside the hammer mill, they would back up onto the southern most threshing floor of the barn and blow the ground feed into a wooden storage bin on the southern most side of the threshing floor in the barn. This bin had a chute that dropped through the floor and into a feed box in the south feed entry, what we called the second feed entry.

Other grains such as wheat, rye, soybeans, and perhaps shelled corn were stored in the granary. The cats loved the granary as a place to dig and make their deposits.

A Sensenig's Hammer Mill Truck similar to one that visited our farm.

A picture of the second hideout with Kiefer, my son, standing in it before renovations.

Later, one of the granary's compartments was used to start chickens in the cool spring since it was sheltered and received some southern heat.

By the 1980s, the granary saw little use; my father built a huge metal grain bin toward the south eastern corner of the barn. The dais for this grain bin is all that remains.

In The Secret Places

. As kids, Doug and I used the northern most overhang of the barn as one of our hideouts. We would play and tinker in the room during the summer and in our free time. I can remember Doug rigging up a car radio with a plug which he took into our bedroom, so that we could listen the the Phillies' ballgames.

A second, less accessible hideout was in a southern addition to the barn. From the first floor, we would have to pull ourselves up through a hole in the upper floor. Jason also used this as a hideout. This hideout no longer exists due to renovations on the southern end of the barn.

A Tornado Raises the Roof

When storms thundered and blackened the sky, we often watched them from the porch. Watching the lightening fork and dagger downward was like having one's own fireworks display. Until the road was raised in the 1980s, the front yard would completely flood in the fiercest of these storms. The raging waters delighted us kids, though they typically meant that there was water in our basement which did not thrill my parents quite as much. We would be forced inside if the wind blew to much rain onto the porch.

It was around 1980 when one such storm had forced us inside. My parents were upstairs getting ready to go somewhere. I was downstairs in the wallpapered living room, watching the storm through the eastern windows, which looked out toward the barn. I watched the sheeting rain slant southward by the wind. A particularly strong gust obscured the barn. When the gust abated, the northern most part of the barn roof was gone. Panicked I called for parents, yelling "The barn roof is gone."

The main barn roof landed on the field to the south. Rueben Oberholtzer also had a section of roof come off his barn, and land in the middle of West Metzler Road. Many years later, I wrote the following poem recounting this experience:

OFF KILTER

When the thunderheads rolled frantic from the North
Armed with gales, sounding like a full-throttled
locomotive,
I stared through the window as the rain sheeted
down.
The violent wind shivered the trees.
The world on the verge of going off kilter.

After the dark clouds spent themselves and the
tormenting rains lifted,
The front yard maple lush with summer sprawled
across the road, garnished with dancing wires.
Chunks of jagged asphalt and black mailboxes

Photos of the barn disaster in 1980. Above: The northern section of the barn with roof missing. The extension off the back of the barn was also missing its roof. Below: A view from the back of the bar shows the roof of the extension balanced precariously and the crushed wire corn crib.

accented the front yard.
The barn's tin hat bathed in the corn stubble mud;
Much of the field now painted the white-skinned
barn.
The world was off kilter.
The world was off——

Dry Wells on the Farm

When we first moved onto the farm, the barn and the house drew water from the same well, a well that sat to the southwest of the house. This may not have been a problem for Jacob and Elmer and the cattle they raised, but when our family grew to six and we had 50 head of cattle in the barnyard, this became more of an issue. The problem came to a head one hot summer. The grass in the front lawn was withering; the property's lone well just could not provide the water needed. This was the only summer I can remember using the outhouse behind the house. It stood where the chicken house and the storage shed met on the south side. All that remains today is the step leading into where the outhouse once stood.

A second well was drilled about 30 feet southwest of the original well pit. These two wells still provide the water for the house. Another well was drilled about thirty feet to the south of the hand dug well, and it supplies water to the barn and the Hertzog Homestead Bed and Breakfast Carriage House Suites. No one is quite sure when the hand dug well ceased operations.

Shenanigans Around the Homestead House

Growing up, my parents always heated the house with wood and oil. The wood fireplace was located in the southwest corner of the den. The den was on the first floor, the south-east room. Wood was cut from the wooded area on the south-west corner of the farm. I can still remember dad backing up the blue pickup truck to the side porch. Dad gave Doug and I the job stacking the wood on the porch so that we could easily access it during the cold winter months. One time in particular, we were unloading the truck and stacking the wood, when one of us tossed a log in through the kitchen window. It landed in my mother's frying pan. I found this particularly funny. Unfortunately, it was not the only house window we broke.

I was 21 at the time. My mom had left my Jason and I at home alone one Saturday morning. Doug was at college; Jessica lived in her own apartment by this time.

Somewhere in the course of the morning, my youngest brother and I began to fight. Knowing me, I probably started it. I chased him around the kitchen, through the den, and then out the Indian door, which I locked as he exited. I then ran to the laundry room and locked the side porch door as well, effectively barring him out of the house.

Keeping his cool, he pretended it did not matter. He went out to feed the pigs and the sheep. I eventually unlocked the doors. When he came in, it was like nothing had ever happened. For a little while at least.

We began to fight again. This time I was the one being pursued. As I darted out the Indian door and onto the front porch, I heard the lock slide shut, and I knew what Jason had planned. He was going to lock me out of the house returning the favor. I moved right and took the corner of the house at a run, heading for the side porch door.

I headed through the door, with my left arm outstretched as he flung it shut. The door had two two by one foot panes of glass. My splayed fingers punched through the glass, shards scattering across the laundry floor. The door hit the door frame, dragging fragments along my arm as it closed. It bounced back off the frame, impaling the shards still attached to the door window frame into my bicep.

For years afterwards, I had small pieces of glass in my arm. I never received stitches, but I did receive a reaming out from mom and dad when they arrived home.

My Mother's Garden

We were not a wealthy family. My mother, a competent seamstress, made most of our clothing and raised the bulk of the food we ate. The garden lay to the south of the house and extended south towards the fields, and was framed in by the butcher house to the east and the rolling machine shed to the west. We raised limas, string beans, snap peas, sweet potatoes, white potatoes, red beets, celery, carrots, corn, tomatoes, raspberries, strawberries, lettuce, and much more.

I never enjoyed woking in the garden when I was kid, though I learned a lot in the process that came back to me when I decided to garden in my adult life. I remember measuring out rows with my mother and father, holding the string at one end as they hoed a furrow along it into the ground, and then placed the seeds one inch a part into the row. When my brother and I were sent to hoe and weed the garden, it usually resulted in us throwing dirt clumps at each other. The same happened when we harvested tomatoes or thinned peaches on the peach tree that stood a few feet away from where the garden stood. These fruits became our assault weapons by which we antagonized each other. Many welts were received during these battles.

I remember my mother also paying us 1 cent for every potato beetle we picked off the potatoes and crushed.

Picking peas and limas was back breaking work. Walking through the corn rows with a wooden half-bushel basket was not fun either in the damp early morning of a hot, muggy August day. The pollen from the tassels was extremely itchy. Mom often promised that if we worked hard in the mornings, she would give us the afternoons off.

Mom canned and froze most of what we raised. I can vividly remember the hissing and chittering of the canner as it preserved our produce. Potatoes were stored in the root cellar under the summer kitchen.

We actually had two orchards on the property: one behind the house which had a few apple trees, peach trees, a plum tree, grapes, and a sour cherry tree, and another to the south on a flat area near the hill that contained apple trees, a pear tree, and some peach trees. We went through tons of peaches, pears, and apples in our family.

Playing in the Front Yard

I remember playing ghost in the graveyard in our front lawn, and playing baseball with my brothers and dad. We had ghost men hold the bases when we played, since we were short players. With my dad, we only had four players. The steps to the front porch functioned a first base, the cistern furtherest away from the house was second[1], and the pole the held up the electric wire that ran from the barn to the house was third base.

We also climbed the maple tree near the road which had a fork in one branch, making it the perfect place to sit. This tree also got us into trouble. From the branches we tested the adage of cats always landing on their feet. Our neighbor Mary Jane Oberholtzer recalls Doug and I deciding that we wanted to bring our black cocker spaniel Chip and Dale the Third into the tree with us. We decided the easiest way to do this was to tie a rope to his collar and pull him up. She made a quick call to our mom, which ended the endeavor. We also occasionally climbed the locust tree at the south end of the lawn, but because the bark was rough and the branches not as easy to reach, this happen less often. Years later as an adult, our neighbor and landscaper James Martin, also know as Happy James, identified the tree as a Kentucky coffee tree and not the locust we always grew up calling it.

Other memories of the front lawn were watching fireflies light up the spring evenings from the front porch; we would run to mom who would give us a glass mayonnaise jar and punch holes in the lid. Then, we would dash through the lawn collecting them. Many nights we would fall asleep to the winking fireflies from the jars beside our beds.

I have one other memory of the front lawn. I can remember a time when I was very young that I raced dad down the front lawn from the sidewalk to the locust tree. He was fast. No one could run like him. I can still see him running beside me in his gray work slacks and plaid shirt. In later years as he became older, gained weight, and developed knee problems, this became a memory I went back to. In my child's mind, he ran like the wind.

Bats in the Attic

There were bats that lived in the attic of the summer kitchen and the southern chimney. In the early evening they would dart out and sweep over our yard. We would hurl little pebbles up at them causing them to swoop down thinking these were tiny insects. Occasionally one would somehow find its way into the house which would thrill mom to no end. I can still see dad chasing one out a window with a broom as it darted back and forth in the upstairs hall way. This happened only once when I moved back into the house as an adult.

Kristen, my wife, was in Haiti on a mission trip, and I was lying in our bed asleep. I heard something fluttering around my head. I awoke and lay there for a moment until I saw it flash by the window backlit from the outdoor nightlight. The bat had flown down the chimney of the master bedroom and out through the fire place. I wish I could say I bravely went after it, but if memory serves me, I hid under the covers for about ten minutes until I got the nerve to roll out of bed and dash for the door. I did go back in after it, but by then it must have found its way out

The Jacob Metzler Planation in 1994.

through the chimney. My next house project was to seal that chimney.

Playing on Metzler Road

My siblings and I used to sled down the road in winter. The dip West Metzler Road made by our house was steeper then; our runner sleds moved faster. Rueben Oberholtzer remembers a time when my brother Doug and I were standing on our sled at the top of the hill, trying to figure out how to sled standing up without killing ourselves. That we are both still alive is testament that we did not, though sometimes I wonder how we avoided it.

My siblings and I used to race up and down the road on our bikes over this same area. We would often ride our bikes around the Metzler's Mennonite Church parking lot as well. One day Jessica, Doug, and I were riding our bikes up and down the road. We pulled out of the church parking lot, and wheeled down the hill toward Reuben and Mary Jane's house, pedaling as fast as we could. I rode atop of the Green Mean Machine, a lime green bike we received from my Aunt Esther and Uncle Paul Weaver. It had belonged to my cousin Glen.

I always wanted to be first, a trait as an adult I look back on and am not proud of. This trait got me into trouble here. I was determined to be the fastest and first up the other hill. As we pedaled down the hill, I pulled out toward the center of the road and began to edge my way past my sister Jess. As I pulled alongside her, a cattle truck pulled out of the Oberholtzer driveway. My sister panicked, and turned to into our drive way. I slammed my bike into her's, ending in tangle of metal and blood. The cattle truck turned and headed away from us. I still have a scar on my foot from this accident until this day.

You Can't Take The Farm Out Of The Farmer

Sometime in the early 1990s, my mother and father decided to give up farming. It was not an easy decision. My father loved the land; however, the farm had been losing money in the years prior, and it was a consensual and practical decision. The 60 foot silo was torn down, the metal grain bin behind the barn sold, the wire corn cribs dismantled, and much of the equipment sold.

In the early 2000s, my parents built a house on the corner of the farm by High Road and Metzler Road. My wife and I moved onto the farm in the summer of 2003.

Although my father no longer lived on the farm, the land remained a part of him. He loved and cared for his ponds and gardens. Many evenings and Saturdays would find him mowing the water ways. For many years after officially quitting farming, my father set aside an acre or two to plant corn and work the fields. If I ever needed help with something on the farm, he was there.

My father, Kenneth Buch Hertzog, died on December 13th, 2012, a Thursday, around 9:30 in the morning of a heart attack. It was a shock, though not wholly unexpected. He was a heavy man, and the Hertzog family had a history of heart disease.

My parents had the sunroom built over the old side porch into the late 1990s. After his passing, I would stare out the sunroom window of our home, expecting dad to go ambling by on his golf cart, steering it up the causeway by Bella's pasture in a journey to go feed his gold fish. Bella was my daughter's horse for many years.

Other times he would slowly drive by on Metzler Road in his black pickup truck as he always did, smile, and wave on his way home or on his way to unlock the church. He functioned as a caretaker at Metzler's Mennonite Church for many years.

One of my last memories of my father was the Tuesday before he died. I had gone to pick up my son Kiefer from my parents' house. They would often watch my son on Tuesdays. As I was leaving, dad pulled in and waved for me to wait. I had forgotten my hunting knife in his truck. We had gone down to PPL hunting area just west of Conestoga near the Observation Point in southern Lancaster County. He slide it across the top on my red Jetta and then asked if I was doing anything that night. He needed help moving a treadmill. I told him that if he needed help to give me a call, but that I did have friends coming over that night. He never called, but that was not necessarily surprising. He never wanted to inconvenience us. I talked to him briefly after that, on Wednesday when I called to asked mom about how to preserve the sweet potatoes she had given us.

The last time I spent any significant time with him was on that prior Saturday when we had gone hunting. There was never much chit chat when we hunted. We discussed about where we thought we would hunt on the drive down. We hunted separately and then at 11:30 AM headed home. Hunting was one of those things I did just to be near my father.

When we arrived back at my parent's house, we ate lunch. My mother, wife, brother Jason, Jessica, and my Aunt Verna Zimmerman were in the middle of our annual Christmas cookie bake. My father and I went out to move a basketball hoop which he had bought at a sale, so that his grandchildren could play basketball on the driveway. We then went his pole shed, got on his golf cart, and went to check out the rolling machine shed that sitting in disrepair near one of the farm's woods. I was planning to pull it back to the barn to use for chickens that were being shipped to me through the mail that following April.

A funny thing happened as we rode the golf cart around the farm. As we neared a little bank between our houses, that ran ran up to the road beside where the lime kiln was, he floored the golf cart and tried going up it. The ground was too wet and the golf cart started slipping. He let it drift back and then gunned it forward again, dumping pumpkins, gourds and Indian corn he had sitting in a tub on the back seat. It was kind of funny.

Imprinted for Life

I wrote poem about growing up on the farm I will include here.

IMPRINT

When out from Lancaster's womb,
my mother wrapped me
in a patchwork quilt of tobacco, corn, and barley fields. Her manicured
geranium and marigold beds
hemmed in my playpen yard.

Years later, when cicadas chittered and whirred
from the locust and the maple in stereo,
their empty nymph shells became imagination's playthings;
my hand skimmed them across the dry-summer grass to other
worlds.

Armed with a mason jar in the settling evening,
I pursued fireflies;

white cats leapt pirouettes after their dying glow.
Bats dove kamikaze style
toward hurled stone missiles in their path.

Those nights, camping tentless in the shadowed yard,
my back pressed against sheets soaked in the dank-dew grass, the starry
night speckled through the concord arbor leaves.
Along with the Pleiades, those seven sisters,
I heard the bullfrog's deep croak from my father's pond
and the crickets chirping in the cocklebur brush
warn as I drifted off to sleep,
"Do not forget us.
Do not forget."

How This Connects to the Hertzog Homestead

Kenneth Buch Hertzog's family marked two hundred years of the Metzler family presence on the plantation. On the farm, he built the a sixty foot silo and added a grain silo. These both were built and dismantled during his lifetime; the corn cribs that Elmer and Jacob had built were also dismantled. The chicken house behind the homestead house was torn down. In the mid-1990s, my father left farming because it was no longer financially viable. Farming remained in his blood the rest of his life.

The Kenneth Buch Hertzog Family Tree

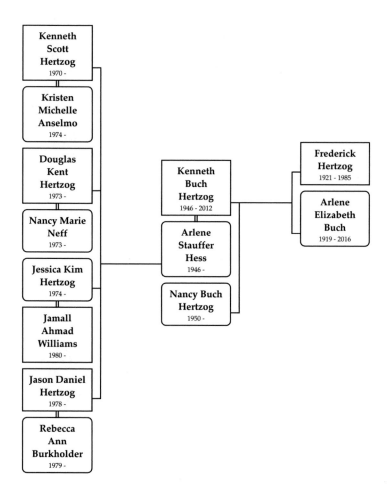

Kenneth Scott Hertzog: The Beginning of the Hertzog Homestead Bed and Breakfast

The Marathon of Life

My sneakers slap the macadam as I jog down West Metzler Road at the beginning of a short run. I am training for the my eighth marathon. To my left, the brick walls of Metzler's Mennonite Church slide past. Many descendants of Jacob Metzler have attended here and many still do. My mother still attends, and my family does. It was Jacob Metzler the second who granted to land to the church, so that the Society of Mennonites could build their initial log structure. Daniel Buch and my father also donated land for the the church to expand. Many Metzler descendants have served as trustees, treasurers and ministers in this church. I, myself, learned a great deal there and have fond memories of growing up and learning about God under its roof.

To my right, a black fence hems in the Metzler's Mennonite Cemetery. Jacob Metzler's family cemetery is contained within, where he buried one of his first children. He and his wife are buried here as are many Metzler descendants. Indeed, all the Metzlers, Buchs, and Hertzogs that lived in the Jacob Metzler Plantation are all buried here. When I was growing up, my father, brothers and I served as caretakers for this cemetery, mowing and weed eating around the head stones.

As I approach North Farmersville Road, Metzler's one room schoolhouse perches on the corner. Barbara and Lizzie Metzler attended here, as did Jacob, Harry, and Elmer Metzler Buch, my grandmother, and many other descendants of the Jacob Metzler clan. This school was a public school until 1964, when it was sold at auction, bought by the plain community, and opened as a private school. The Oberholtzers, our neighbors, attended here. We were invited and watched many Christmas programs, with students reciting poetry, stories, and plays. We joined with the Plain community as they sang Christmas hymns in German.

John B. Horning, another descendant of Jacob N. Metzler, shares what it was like during its last years as a public school. Mrs. Griffiths, a graying heavy-set woman who loved teaching, commanded the classroom, a classroom which had students ranging from first to eighth grade and six to thirteen years of age. The second bell, which was rung by a student, sounded at 8:30 AM and indicated all students were to be in their seats.

She started class by reading a short passage from scripture and then having everyone stand up an recite the Lord's Prayer. After this, students gathered around the piano and she led the school in singing some fun songs. From there, students went to work, with first graders reading in one area and others working in spelling and grammar workbooks in another. The drone of busyness was constant in the room.

After lunch at 11:30, during which some students ran home to eat, Mrs. Griffiths would instruct the students in history, geography, health, and art. Students would sometimes practice for a poetry recital or explore the bookmobile which would occasionally drop by to resupply the school's limited library. At the end of the day, student's carried out ashes from the stove in the cellar, clapped erasers, swept the floor, emptied and burned the trash, and refilled the drinking water in the crock.[1]

The Metzler's One Room School House

My run curves down past Elias Moyer's miller's house that still stands near the road. The mill has been long gone, its most recent incarnation torn down in 1976. A right onto Turtle Hill Road takes me past where Conestoga Park once stood, now known as the Conestoga Campgrounds. The trolley once ran through here. The singing, the dancing, and the roller skating rink have been long gone though the buttresses where the trolley once crossed the creek remain.

My right onto High Road, originally called Trolley Road, takes me past the stone quarries. Stone was originally mined here for the trolleys and perhaps for use in building and expanding the Jacob Metzler Plantation.

I cannot run without seeing the rich heritage, the legacy, and the impact that my ancestors, the people who lived and helped birth the Jacob Metzler Plantation, had on this community. I hope in some way that I and my family am able to have a similar legacy.

My Journey Away from the Plantation

Though I grew up on the farm and now reside on the farm, I did not always live there. Through a program called Youth Evangelism Service, I lived in Philadelphia and Baltimore and also Mexico, Guatemala, and Italy. I lived in Hesston, Kansas when I attended Hesston College where I earned my Liberal Arts Degree and explored agriculture, music, and drama.

Although my family lived in the Conestoga Valley School District, I attended Eastern Lancaster County High School (known to the locals as Garden Spot) because they had a vocational agriculture program. The Future Farmers of America, as well as 4-H, were core components of my life growing up, and had us scurrying to the Ephrata Fair, the New Holland Fair, and even the Harrisburg Farmshow to show steers, pigs, and heifers.

When I left Lancaster County to attend Hesston College for Agriculture Engineering, I had no plans to come back and live permanently in Lancaster County. After graduating from Hesston, my dreams were to buy a 2000 acre ranch in Montana. I had investigated land prices near Billings and was mesmerized by the landscape.

In 1991, I lived for four months off the edge of a garbage dump in Zona Seis in Guatemala City, Guatemala. I was a member of a Youth Evangelism Service team lead by Carol Bollinger. While living there, I taught English, and it was this experience that led me back to Lancaster County, to Millersville University, to teach at Solanco School District and later at Penn Manor School District, and eventually back to the farm.

My first day at Hesston College, Hesston, Kansas in August of 1990.

Kristen Michele Anselmo: The New Jersey Invasion

Kristen Michelle Anselmo was born on Februray 2, 1974 in Perth Amboy, New Jersey to Paul Joseph Anselmo and Diana Ratti Rosner. Her father's side descended from Sicilian farmers in Caccamo, Italy. In 2001 and in 2017, we had the pleasure of visiting the area her family was from, and even saw the chalk kilns on the family farm. Because they were poor farmers, family information beyond the 1800s is difficult to obtain.

Her mother's side was descended from Italian and Hungarian Jews in Northern Italy. The Rattis can be traced back to the 1300s, mostly due to Kristen being a fourth cousin to Pope Pius the XI. It is ironic that my wife is a relative to the Pope and I am a descendant of Martin Luther the Reformer.

Diana's father was a collaborator in the underground against Mussolini during World War II. He was caught, escaped to Cuba, and then came to the United States.

Kristen's growing up years were spent 166 Prospect Avenue in Edison, New Jersey. She was the oldest of three, followed by first Kevin and then Mark. Her parents were nominally Catholic, but had a salvation experience, and they attended several protestant churches. Kristen attended Timothy Christian School.

Because of her dyslexia and attention deficit disorder, she struggled academically in school, spending many summers attending summer school. But in theater and dance she excelled.

166 Prospect Avenue, Edison, NJ where Kristen grew up.

When she was 16, she traveled to Haiti with Abundant Life Christian Center. This trip revolutionized her life. The group she traveled with worked in Cite Sole, Haiti, the poorest city in the Western Hemisphere. While she was walking down one of the sewer filled streets, a Haitian woman ran up to her, dropped a bundle into her arms, and dashed off. When the bundle of cloth began to move, Kristen panicked. The woman had dropped a baby girl into her arms.

Kristen started screaming for help, shouting to her group, "This woman just handed me a baby and ran away!" Some men in her group ran after the lady and caught her. When they brought her back, she was weeping. When the men asked why she had done this, she said that if the child was with the American, she would have a better life.

This experience led her to know in her heart that she would one day adopt a little girl from Haiti. In 1999, she and her friend

Curt Edwards led a short-term mission team of Sight and Sound Theatre employees to Haiti. This resulted in a series of short-term mission trips over the subsequent years. Haiti Connection Network, now a part of Life Connection Missions, was established by Kristen and Curt out of these trips. This also resulted in the adoption of my lovely daughter, Taicha Alphonse Hertzog.

In 1992, after Kristen had graduated high school, she landed a job at Sight and Sound as Pilate's wife in *Behold the Lamb*. She went on to work there for over 13 years. However, this was not the first time she was in Lancaster. Her family had traveled from Edison, New Jersey to Lancaster many times over her growing up years. She loved the Amish, sometimes even dressing up as one of them.

Our Meeting in Splendor

I met Kristen as a direct result of growing up on the farm. In 1993, I was employed as an Animal Handler at Sight and Sound Theaters, where my role hitching up and driving horses on and off stage for the production of *The Splendor of Easter*.

Trained as an actress, Kristen fulfilled many roles in this production, but the most memorable one to me was when I interacted with her in the town scene. As I guided an old chestnut mare, a flapping jawed Debbie, across the stage with her cart hitched behind her, I would doff my cap her direction, and she, looking beautiful in her pink victorian style dress complete with pink parasol, would curtsey back.

Two years later, after I had left Sight and Sound Theatres and worked for UPS, our paths crossed once again. I met her at Petra Christian Fellowship in New Holland, PA. At the time, I was leading worship Sunday nights for a weekly young adult event called Life Spring. She was leading the drama team called Potter's Wheel. I remember seeing her one Sunday and recognizing her from my time at Sight and Sound. Decked out in a white dress with a white summer hat, she waltzed up the church

Our wedding on August 18, 1996. Picture was taken in the front of Metzler's Mennonite Church. From left to right: Jessica Hertzog, Kevin Anselmo, Kendra Halman, Jason Hertzog, Pamela Ogershock, Kristen Anselmo, Scott Hertzog, Tara Glickman, Brent Martin, Lynn Kauffman, Doug Hertzog, and Mark Anselmo.

aisle to a seat that a friend was holding for her in the front. My first thought at seeing here was "what a snob!"

A month or two later, Kristen invited members of the Life Spring team to come see the show *The Eternal Flame* at Sight and Sound. It was a Saturday night in September 1995. We went out to Denny's Restaurant on Route 30 afterward. I attended the show with my parents, and she invited me out afterward with the youth group from Petra. On the way to drop me off at my house, she asked me out. I was dumbfounded. I had never had a girl ask me out before. Playing it cool, I told her I would think about it, but my heart was pounding in anticipation. The next day I called her and scheduled our first date. We ended up at the Italian Oven, a restaurant that no longer exists, sipping soda through pasta straws and talking. By December, we were engaged.

Kristen Anselmo Hertzog wedding photo taken oat Harold and Verna Zimmerman's farm on August 18, 1996.

I remember clearly our third date, the date that Kristen met my family. Our cultures were very different. She had grown up in a demonstrative, Italian family from New Jersey. I grew up in a reserved, Germanic Mennonite family, one in which people rarely spoke their minds. She grew up on artichokes, cannoli, and pasta dishes; I grew up on mashed potatoes, chicken, and lima beans. That evening, when we sat down with my family to eat, my family quietly bowed their heads, as did I. We always said a silent prayer. Unfortunately, I forgot to clue Kristen in on this. In sync, we would bow our heads to pray, and then, as if there were some kind of psychic connection, we would raise our heads, indicating the prayer was over. This baffled Kristen.

We were married on August 18, 1996, a Sunday afternoon. At our ceremony we blended customs from both our families. Gene Zoll, pastor at Metzlers, and Lester Zimmerman, pastor at Petra Christian Fellowship, conducted the ceremony, which included a traditional foot washing ceremony.

For those of you not familiar with this practice, Jesus practiced this at the last supper, taking on the stance of a servant. At the appointed time in our ceremony, my best man and brother, Jason Hertzog, brought out a basin filled with water (and a rubber ducky which he humorously put in). Hip to floor length towels were wrapped around our waists as we, in turn, knelt before each other and washed each other's feet. This was a symbol of our pledge to serve each other.

Our Journey Back to the Plantation

Because of my passion for farming, I initially went to Hesston College to earn an Agricultural Engineering degree. I thought that when I left my parent's farm, I would never be back. I switched my major to drama and music the next semester, and finally ended my time there with a liberal arts degree. I eventually graduated from Millersville University with an Bachelors in English Education and took a teaching position at Solanco High School.

After we married in 1996, we lived on 140 W. Main St., in Strasburg, above where the weekly Strasburg News was printed for over one hundred years.

I taught ninth and tenth grade English at Solanco School

4 Genrations from Left to Right: Kenneth Buch Hertzog, Kenneth Kiefer Hertzog, Arlene Elizabeth Hertzog, and Kenneth Scott Hertzog.

District for four years. After this, Kristen and I felt called to Italy and spent some time in there with the YES program. After Italy, Kristen and I moved back to the Strasburg area, knowing that in a few years we would be moving onto the farm.

None of my other brothers and sisters wanted the farm. After Italy, I acquired an English Teaching position at Penn Manor High School, where I still work today. I eventually went on to earn a masters degree in English from West Chester University.

I, along with my wife Kristen, bought the farm and 23 acres from my parents in 2003. My father and mother retained the rest of the acreage.

It is a weird feeling moving back into the place where I grew up, where so many memories were made. As an adult and married to someone who did not grow up in the house, we needed to make the house our own. Never-the-less, tearing down

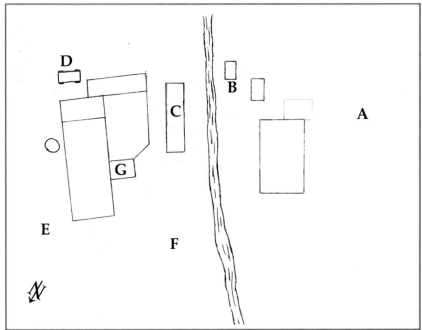

A. The chicken house and the shed no longer exist; the shed had fallen into disrepair and after the the chickens were moved to the rolling machine shed, my father tore the entire structure down. B. We built a small shed over the original 40-foot hand-dug well in order to keep children and guests from inadvertently falling in. C. Pole shed is torn down and rebuilt as the Hertzog Homestead's Carriage House Suites. D. Rolling machine shed is rescued from the fields and relocated here to again house chickens. E. The two round wire corn cribs no longer exist, with one being torn down after the tornado and the other after my father no longer farmed. F. Garage is torn down by my father, making it easier to see when pulling out of the driveway. G. This addition to the barn is torn down because it is leaning. This exposes the original forebay and displays the front of the barn as it existed in Jacob Metzler's time.

wall paper and redoing floors felt like the we were desecrating a sacred place in some way.

Despite my love and appreciation of the land, I had little interest in actually farming it. Instead, we rented out the land to Crystal Springs Farms as my father also did, and then later to Chris High. Corn and soybeans remained staple crops along with some winter rye.

We had few animals in the early years of living there. We had a Jack Russel Terrier named Petey and a few indoor and outdoor cats. After Petey died, we obtained a rust colored dog named

Rusty and a Welsh Corgey Mix called Macy. Around 2010, we bought a large pony called Bella for my daughter as a Christmas present.

My son, Kenneth Kiefer Hertzog, the ninth generation of Metzler's to live in the house, was born on April 26, 2007. He was followed by our daughter who was adopted on April 15, 2009. She was born in Port-au-Prince, Haiti on November 24, 2001.

Taicha eating sugar cane in 2008.

The Evolution of the Farm

In the Spring of 2008, a storm knocked down the Kentucky Coffee tree that had towered over the original well pit for years. This tree is pictured in the earliest photos of the farm. The southern end of the lawn looked empty with out it, though recent years some of its saplings have begun to grow and sprout out.

An extension that jutted out the front of the barn had begun to noticeably sag and twist over the years. Finally in 2011, I had Lee Sauder remove it. Once again the fore-bay was exposed and stretched across the front of the barn. In 2012, the Northern Gable of the barn was repointed on the outside. And then in the spring of 2013, the southern end extension was rebuilt as the original roof and wood were sagging.

In 2010, a 21 kilowatt solar system was mounted and installed to the south west of the house. This provides almost 85% of our energy needs. Because of my love of the land and nature, this helped make us more environmentally conscience. That same year, central air was installed in the main house.

In 2013, a garden once again graced the property, in a space south of the butcher house. We rescued and rebuilt the rolling machine shed that was falling apart out in

The demise of the Kentucky Coffee tree.

the field. I discovered later that this shed had been sold at the Elmer Buch sale in 1976 but was never picked up. Like it did when I was a child, this shed now houses our chickens.

The butcher house was converted into a cabana for our pool. This later became the head-quarters for the Haitian Connection Network. When the new Carriage House Suites opening up in November of 2015, the became the Hertzog Homestead Bed and Breakfast offices.

The Hope for Haiti Benefit Auction

In 2012, we were actively involved in higher education and self-sustainability measures in Haiti through our work in Haitian Connection Network. In fall of 2011, along with the encouragement of family and friends, we decided to utilize our farm in an effort to raise funds for the organizations like the Haitian Connection Network to work with young adults in Haiti.

Kristen asked co-workers, neighbors, friends and family to assist them with hosting a benefit auction in spring of 2012. The request was met with overwhelming support from the local community, and we saw the English and the Plain community

The Hope for Haiti Benefit Auction in 2014 behind the Hertzog Homestead barn.

come together in this effort. The combined efforts and hours of volunteers brought in auction tents, children's games, a professional auction company, and food and other donated items. Funds went towards the work in Haiti.

Over the past years, various nonprofit organizations working in Haiti with a focus on education and self-sustainability have benefited from this auction. The Haitian Connection Network, Life Connection Mission, Haiti Partners, and Christian Aid Ministries are just a few of the many.

It remains our goal to continue to help those in need and to help the less fortunate. At the Hertzog Homestead Bed and Breakfast, the auction is one of the ways we can do this.

The Hertzog Homestead Bed and Breakfast

Like my ancestors, we have evolved the plantation to meet the changing world and times. My wife and I started the The Hertzog Homestead Bed and Breakfast in 2003. People have traveled from as faraway as Australia, Italy, and South Africa to enjoy the peace and quiet of the area and to appreciate the rolling

The plantation house as it exists today.

hills of the farmland. When we originally started the bed and breakfast, we had one suite in the main house, in the oldest part of the house called the Historic Metzler Suite. We originally had another upstairs room with a shared bath that we rented out. This was the original Daniel Buch room. When we began the process of adopting our daughter, we took this room back and made it our daughter's bedroom.

In 2014 the pole barn that stood between the Sweitzer barn

The Carriage House Suites

A ariel photograph of the Hertzog Homestead Bed and Breakfast (The Jacob Metzler Plantation) taken on August 9, 2014. The building between the barn the main plantation house has since been converted into the Carriage House Suites.

and the plantation house was torn down. It had been added onto at both ends and modified so much that it had lost much of its historical significance. When we tore it down, there was a 16 by 14 stone foundation. The purpose of this original building is unknown, but perhaps it functioned as the original carriage house for the plantation in its early years.

The building that took its place became known as the Carriage House Suites because of this. This building added three additional rooms to our bed and breakfast: the Meyer Suite, the Buch Suite, and the Hertzog Suite. Every family who has ever lived on this planation is represented in the rooms of the Hertzog Homestead. Elva Oberholtzer, my sixth cousin and our neighbor, cooks for our bed and breakfast. She finally has her own kitchen, which we call Elva's Kitchen, in the Carriage House Suites.

The Hertzog Homestead Event Venue

As the years went by, concerns arose over the deterioration of the barn. Farming had evolved over the past 25 years making my much of my agricultural knowledge irrelevant. I could no longer see myself taking on that role. Together, my wife and I decided to repurpose the 1765 Sweitzer barn as an event venue, allowing us to hold wedding receptions, corporate events, and other special functions.

I still wanted it to feel and look much like it had for the past 250 years. Stone walls were repointed, and Lee Sauder helped shore up and re-lay the goliath, axe-hewn floor planks. As I was cleaning out the filthy granary, it was as if a voice from the past spoke. I uncovered a granary slat that had Jacob N. Metzler's name stenciled across it (see page 54). That granary slat can now be seen near the top of the north gable wall.

The last wedding ceremony occurred on our farm in 1884 when my great-grandfather, Daniel Buch married Elizabeth Metzler, Jacob N. Metzler's great-granddaughter. On June 3rd, 2017, 133 years later, a wedding ceremony once again graced the property of the Hertzog Homestead Event Venue.

How This Connects to the Hertzog Homestead

My objective while living on the plantation of Jacob Metzler has been to preserve the farm's history and structures the best I can. The northern gable of the barn has been internally and externally repointed along with the external facade of the front wall. A southern addition to the barn was rebuilt. The rolling machine shed of Daniel Buch was falling apart in the fields and was rescued and rebuilt. It now houses our young chickens. The original carriage house had been cobbled together over the years so that only a foundation was original; we tore that building down and rebuilt the Carriage House suites as a part of the Hertzog

Homestead Bed and Breakfast.

The Kenneth Scott Hertzog Family

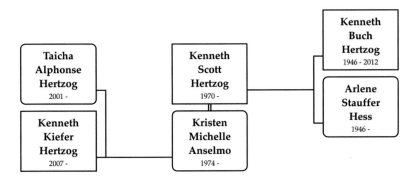

K. Scott Hertzog

Final Thoughts

I am immensely honored and humbled to be living on the land of my ancestors. I realize how unique this is in today's generation. It is my hope that the work that both Kristen and I put into the Jacob Metzler Plantation will continue its legacy and honor the traditions that have been set forth in years past.

There is no doubt the growing up on a farm such as this is a lot of work, but it is also extremely rewarding. It is a wonderful place for my children to grow up, to run outside, and play. To understand the cycle of life and where their food comes from. It is also place we can get outside have peace away from the distractions of technology.

The rolling farmland is beautiful. It is the perfect place to think, sit on the porch, and watch the world go by.

Author Scott Hertzog, Kiefer Hertzog, Taicha Hertzog, and Kristen Anselmo Hertzog. Picture was taken in Caccamo, Sicily in 2017.

ABOUT THE AUTHOR

Kenneth Scott Hertzog currently resides with his wife Kristen and their two children, Taicha and Kiefer, on the Jacob Metzler Plantation, now known as the Hertzog Homestead Bed and Breakfast. While he is employed as an English Teacher at Penn Manor High School, he maintains a connection to his farming heritage by raising poultry, maintaining a garden, and genealogical research.

After graduating from Garden Spot High School, he attended Hesston College, Hesston, Kansas, where he received a Liberal Arts Associates Degree. He then attended Millersville University where he received a Bachelor's of Science Degree in Secondary Education and was certified to teach English. Afterwards he attended West Chester University where he received his English Masters degree with an emphasis in creative writing.

K. Scott Hertzog

End Notes

Chapter 1: A Time Before Settlers

1. Kinsey, Dr. W. Fred. *Lower Susquehanna Valley Prehistoric Indians.* 1977.
2. Kinsey.
3. Kinsey.
4. Kinsey.
5. Wallace, Paul A.W. *Indians in Pennsylvania. Commonwealth of Pennsylvania.* Harrisburg. 1989.
6. Kent, Barry C. *Susquehanna's Indians.* Commonwealth of Pennsylvania. Pennsylvania Historical and Museum Commission. 2001.
7. *Lancaster County Pennsylvania: a History.* Editor: H.M.J. Klein, Ph. D., Lewis Historical Publishing Company, Inc., New York. 1924.
8. Wallace, Paul A.W. *Historic Indian Paths of Pennsylvania.* 1952.
9. Kent.
10. Kent.

Chapter 2: It begins With Elias

1. Friesen, Steve. *A Modest Mennonite Home.* Good Books, Intercourse, PA. 1990.
2. "Eppingen." *Wikipedia.* Feb. 23, 2013.
3. Based on research I did, I have Elias Meyer's birthday as 11 Dec 1697 based on Annette Burgert's research *Emigrants from Eppingen*, p.23. He is also listed with 3 family members when he comes across on the *William and Sarah* in 1727. Only the head of households were listed on the passenger lists on these ships. It seems a logical conclusion that his wife is traveling with him along with his sons Vincent and John. The research of Richard Warren Davis also suggests on Mennosearch.com that Vincent Meyer, born 1721, was the son of Elias. However,

in the article in *Pennsylvania Mennonite Heritage*, Jane Evan Best suggests that Elias Meyer (Labeled MS3341.1) was born around 1710. This date makes it impossible to be Vincent's father and also unlikely that he would have been the head of household traveling with a wife and two children in 1727. She goes on to suggest that John Meyer (MS3341) is Elias's father. The 1710 date makes sense in the way she laid out her line, but obviously if Elias was born on 11 Dec 1697 as my research suggests, then, John who was born in 1784, would be only be 13. I think there is a greater possibility that Elias Meyer is the son of Hans Meyer (MS334) born 1661. Nico P. Kittel, a genealogical and family researcher from Germany, is in agreement with these conclusions, backed up with evidence from *Schweitzer Einwanderer in den Kraichgau*, which analyzed Lutheran Church records, whose pastors recorded Anabaptist marriages they heard of and who buried the Anabaptists in their cemeteries. Some of the information in this book also comes from general records of the Anabaptists secret meetings. Elias Meyer's wife's tombstone also confirms my research.

4. Brobst, William A. "The History of the German Immigration to America." *The Brobst Chronicles*. 1999.
5. Pray, Francis E. "The Palatine Emigration to America" *The Gibbs Magazine*. 2014.
6. Brobst.
7. Brobst.
8. Brobst.
9. Myers, Cheryl. "Ship William and Sarah." *Immigrant Ships Transcribers Guild*. 2001.
10. "The German immigration into Pennsylvania through the port of Philadelphia from 1700 to 1775 : part II: The Redemptioners." University of Toronto Library
11. Information on what it was like to arrive in Philadelphia comes from lecture by Henry Bennett given at the 275th Metzler Reunion.

12. Bennet Lecture at the 275th Metzler Reunion.
13. Diffenderfer, Frank R. "The Three Earls."
14. Brobst.
15. The warrant is recorded in Volume A, number 11, page 445. The survey is copied in book C 121, Page 197. The number of the warrant 128.
16. Brobst.
17. "Winter of 1741 was one for the history books." *Pennsylvania Gazette*, April 9, 1741.
18. "Old Landmark Being Demolished" Article from the School Teacher Thomas Weaver.
19. Richard Bennett & John Elton. *History of Corn Milling* London, Simpkin, Marshall and Company, 1898.
20. Zimmerman, Jane Metzler. *Jacob N. Metzler and His Descendants.* 2013.
21. Richard Bennett & John Elton.
22. Richard Bennett & John Elton.
23. "Old Landmark Being Demolished"
24. "Old Landmark Being Demolished"
25. "Old Landmark Being Demolished"
26. "Wagon Passes Over A Man." *Reading Eagle*, June 13, 1908.
27. "Assaults Aged Couple On Lancaster Farm" *Reading Eagle*. February, 9, 1918.
28. "Berks County Man To Face Murder Charge." *Reading Eagle*. March 20, 1918.
29. "Guilty in Second Degree." *Reading Times*. Reading, PA. 11 September 1918.
30. "Refuse Pardons to Dauphin Men." *The Evening News*. Harrisburg. 28 March 1925.
31. "Stays Granted to Two Slayers." *The Evening News*. Harrisburg. 22 September 1927.
32. "Berks Contain Held for Murder at Lancaster." *The Reading Eagle*. Reading, PA. 21 March 1918.
33. "Old Landmark Being Demolished"
34. Zimmerman, Jane Metzler.

35. Indenture located in Deed Book H, Page 355. Historic Document Archives, Lancaster County Courthouse.
36. Schonewolf, Beverly J. "Elias Myers." *Oviatt, Rockwell, Mather, Myers Ancestry.* 2011.
37. Schonewolf, Beverly J.
38. The Grave monument of Louisa Fredricka Globmann Meyer, located at Bethany Cemetery, Ephrata, Lancaster County, PA. It reads:

H(I)ER LIEGT BEGRABEN
LOWISA FRIDERRICK MEYER
EINE GEBORNE GLOBMANN
SIE WAR GEBOREN ......M....
1699 IN EUROPA IN DER
PFALTZ IN DER STA(D)T ETT...(EPP?)...
IN DER EHE HAT SIE GELEBT
MIT ELIAS MEYER 40 JAHR
UND HAT 16 KINDER GEZEIGT
10 SÖHNE UND 6 TÖCHTER
UND VERSCHIED D. 6. FEBRU(AR)
1759......ALTER.....

Translation:

Here (in this grave) is buried
Louisa Fredericka Meyer
née Globmann
she was born ...M. (*may/march*)...
1699 in Europe, in the
Palatinate, in the town of Ett....(*maybe incorrect, should say 'Eppingen' – but there exists Ettlingen in Germany, too.*)
She lived in marriage
with Elias Meyer for 40 years
and shown (raised) 16 children:
10 sons and 6 daughters
and died on the 6th of February
in 1759 at the age of......

Translation by Nico P. Kittel (March 11, 2016)

Chapter 3: Petter Meyers: The Beginnings of the Hertzog Homestead

1. Schonewolf, Beverly J. "Elias Myers." *Oviatt, Rockwell, Mather, Myers Ancestry.* 2011.
2. Schonewolf, Beverly J. "Elias Myers."
3. Indenture located in Deed Book H, Page 355. Historic Document Archives, Lancaster County Courthouse.
4. Schonewolf, Beverly J. "Peter Myers." *Oviatt, Rockwell, Mather, Myers Ancestry.* 2011.
5. Sauder, David. Editor. *Metzler's Mennonite Congregation: 1728 -1978.* Hocking Printing
   Company, Ephrata, PA 1978.
6. Friesen, Steve. *A Modest Mennonite Home.* Good Books, Intercourse, PA. 1990.
7. Bond, Beverley W., Jr. "The Quit-Rent System in the American Colonies" *The American Historical Review ,* Vol. 17, No. 3 (Apr., 1912), pp. 496-516.
8. Much of my knowledge of barn structure and classification is based on the work of Robert F. Ensminger and his book *The Pennsylvania Barn: Its Origin, Evolution, and Distribution in North America (Creating the North American Landscape)* The Johns Hopkins University Press; second edition edition, March 26, 2003.
9. Ensminger.
10. McMurry and Nancy Van Dolsen, Editors. *Architecture and Landscape of the Pennsylvania Germans, 1720-1920.* University of Pennsylvania Press,
    Philadelphia, Pennsylvania: 2001.
11. Friesen.
12. Chappell, Edward A. "Acculturation in the Shenandoah Valley: Rhenish Houses of the Massanutten Settlement,"

Common Places: Readings in American Vernacular Architecture. Athens, GA. 1986.

13. Friesen.
14. Friesen.
15. Friesen.
16. Friesen.
17. Friesen.
18. Schonewolf, Beverly J. "Peter Myers."
19. McMurry and Nancy Van Dolsen.
20. Friesen.
21. Schonewolf, Beverly J. "Peter Myers."
22. Schonewolf, Beverly J. "Peter Myers."

Chapter 4: The Arrival of the Metzlers

1. Kittel, Nico Patric. Emails exchanged.
2. Kittel.
3. Miller, Erma Metzler. "Metzler Family History." A descendent of John Metzler.
4. Metzler, Lem. "Valentine and Anna Nissley Metzler History" May 15, 2013.
5. Metzler, Lem.
6. Notes from Lem Metzler based on his research.
7. Ruckel, Kraig. *Palatine Emigrants: Emigration from the Rhineland to America - Eigtheenth Century.*
8. Keen, R. Martin. "The Nissley Cemetery in the City of Lancaster, Pennsylvania." *Pennsylvania Mennonite Heritage.* Volume 36, Number 3, July 2013.
9. H. M. J. Klien, Ph. D. *Lancaster County, Pennsylvania: A History* reports this date as June 17, 1763. This is in conflict to Erma Metzler Miller's "Metzler Family History" leaflet, which reports the date of the hail storm as June 17, 1968. She apparently pulled this from the write up on Valentine Metzler from the Mennonite Research Journal published in January of 1968.

10. Brubaker, Jack. "Nissleys, Metzlers, Conestogas." *Lancaster Newspapers*. December 21, 2012.

11. Brubaker.

12. Wiebe, Victor G. "Boehm, Martin (1725-1812)." *Global Anabaptist Mennonite Encyclopedia Online*. December 2012. Web. 23 Jul 2015.

13. Wiebe.

14. Weibe.

15. Hostetter, C. Nelson and E. Morris Sider. "Brethren in Christ Church." Global Anabaptist Mennonite Encyclopedia Online. March 2014. Web. 5 Feb 2016

16. MacMaster, Richard K. *Conscience in Crisis: Mennonites and Other Peace Churches in America, 1739-1789 : Interpretation and Documents (Studies in Anabaptist and Mennonite History).* Herald Press. October 1979.

17. MacMaster, Richard K.

18. MacMaster, Richard K.

19. MacMaster, Richard K.

20. "Historical and Genealogical Sketch of the Metzler Family" Document owned by Jane Metzler Zimmerman.

21. Zimmerman, Jane Metzler. *Jacob N. Metzler and His Descendants*. 2013.

22. Zimmerman, Jane Metzler.

Chapter 5: Jacob N. Metzler and His Plantation

1. Information gathered from Jane Metzler Zimmerman's research on the Hess family.

2. Braght, Theileman J. van. *The Bloody Theater or Martyrs Mirror of the Defenseless Christians who baptized only upon confession of faith, and who suffered and died for the testimony of Jesus, their Saviour, from the time of Christ to the year A.D. 1660.*

3. This date is in conflict with the date mentioned in Jane Metzler Zimmerman's book. My date is pulled from an 1824 Deed between Maria and Christian Metzler to Jacob Metzler.

4. "Lancaster Plain, c. 1730-1960" Agricultural Resources of Pennsylvania.
5. "Lancaster Plain, c. 1730-1960"
6. "Embargo of 1807." The Jefferson Monticello. 2016. Web.
7. Brubaker, Jack. "Trigger was not from around here, but his mother was." *LancasterOnline*. July 16, 2010.
8. From information Kenneth Buch Hertzog had gathered.
9. Zimmerman, Jane Metzler. *Jacob N. Metzler and His Descendants*. 2013.

Chapter 6: Jacob H. Metzler: An Era of Growth and Expansion

1. Story as told by Douglas Hertzog.
2. "Processing Limestone to Make Plaster." *Wabash and Erie Canal Park*. 2009.
3. "Lancaster Plain, c. 1730 - 1960" Agricultural Resources of Pennsylvania, 1700 - 1960.
4. Zimmerman, Jane Metzler. *Jacob Metzler and His Descendants*. 2013
5. Willison, Jim. "Company 'H' 17th Illinois Cavalry" *Illinois in the Civil War*. 2013.
6. Adjutant General's Report 17th Illinois Cavalry Regiment History. Transcribed by Susan Tortorelli. 1997.
7. Willison, Jim.
8. "Metzler's Mennonite Congregation: 1728 - 1978."Edited by David Sauder, 1978.
9. 1850 West Earl Township Records.
10. 1850 West Earl Township Records.
11. 1850 West Earl Township Records.
12. 1860 West Earl Township Records.
13. "Agriculture in the Settlement Period" Agricultural Resources of Pennsylvania, 1700 - 1960.
14. Zimmerman, Jane Metzler. *Jacob Metzler and His Descendants*. 2013

Chapter 7: Jacob S. Metzler: Civil War and Tobacco

1. According to the 1865 deed.
2. The advancement made to Jacob S. Metzler. Courtesy of Jane Metzler Zimmerman.
3. 1870 Tax records.
4. "Lancaster Plain, c. 1730 - 1960" Agricultural Resources of Pennsylvania, 1700 - 1960.
5. A document showing the dissolution of this agreement is in my possession.
6. Herald of Truth, May 1, 1894.
7. Zimmerman, Jane Metzler. *Jacob Metzler and His Descendants*. 2013.
8. Zimmerman, Jane Metzler.

Chapter 8: Daniel and Lizzie Metzler Buch: Telephones, Trolleys, and Farming

1. Based on Mennonite Mutual Aid documents from the 1880s.
2. Ancestry.com. *U.S.,IndexedCounty Land Ownership Maps, 1860-1918* [database on-line]. Provo, UT, USA: Ancestry.com Operations, Inc., 2010. Original data: Various publishers of County Land Ownership Atlases. Microfilmed by the Library of Congress, Washington, D.C.
3. Based on 1908 Journal of John S. Metzler owned by Joann Herr.
4. Information gathered by Kenneth Buch Hertzog.
5. Gingerich, Melvin, Cornelius Krahn, Nanne van der Zijpp and Gerald C. Studer. "Weddings." *Global Anabaptist Mennonite Encyclopedia Online*. 1989. Web. 4 Jan 2016.
6. Beitler, Stu. *PA, NY, DC, KY, MD, IA, TN, RI, FL, GA, MI, MA, KS, SC, IL, NJ, OK Blizzard, Feb 1895* Gen Disasters. October 13th, 2008.
7. 1899 - 1909 Account Books by Daniel W. Buch.
8. Weaver, Jay D. *J. Landis Weaver Autobiography*. 2002.
9. Weaver, Jay D.

10. Zimmerman, Jane Metzler. *Elmer Nolt Metzler & Clara Martin Metzler: Their Commitment to Faith and Family (1897 - 1969)*. Masthoff Press. 2016.
11. Based on oral information from Arlene E. Hertzog, granddaughter of Daniel and Lizzie and on information from Kenneth Buch Hertzog, great-grandson of Daniel and Lizzie.
12. Oral history from Betty White, Brethern Village, Lancaster, PA.
13. May 16, 1913 issue of *The Ephrata Review*. Thanks to Kathy Buch.
14. Shindle, Richard D. "The Conestoga Traction Company." *The Journal of the Lancaster County Historical Society*. Volume 100, Number 3, 1998.
15. *Seeing Lancaster County from a Trolley Window*. Express Printing Company. Lititz. 1909.
16. 1900 Journal by John S. Metzler, owned by Joann Herr.
17. 1900 Journal…
18. Shindle, Richard D. "The Conestoga Traction Company." *The Journal of the Lancaster County Historical Society*. Volume 100, Number 3, 1998.
19. Transparencies, Reflections, Light; Photographic Views of the Cocalico Valley.
20. The Metzler's Trolley Station is mentioned in the "Assaults Aged Couple On Lancaster Farm" *Reading Eagle*. February, 9, 1918 and in an Obituary for Mrs. Aaron Martin who died in 1920 and lived near Metzler's Trolley Station.
21. Transparencies…
22. Sam Oberholtzer grew up next door to the Daniel Buch farm and worked on it in the late 1950's and early 1960's when Jacob and Elmer Metzler Buch owned.
23. The recipes come from my grandmother, Arlene E. Hertzog.

Chapter 9: Jacob and Elmer Metzler Buch: Bachelor Life on the Plantation

1. Based on conversations with the Oberholtzer brothers, Buch family, and my Grandmother. Also referenced in

Zimmerman, Jane Metzler. *Elmer Nolt Metzler & Clara Martin Metzler: Their Commitment to Faith and Family (1897 - 1969).* Masthoff Press. 2016.

2. Based on World War Two Draft Registration cards
3. Sam Oberholtzer was immensely helpful in the gathering of data on what life was like on the farm when Jacob and Elmer lived here.
4. Sam Oberholtzer
5. Sam Oberholtzer
6. Sam Oberholtzer
7. Based on conversations with the Oberholtzer bothers, many of whom worked on the farm in the late 1950s on up through the 1960s.
8. Oral tradition as told by Richard Buch, who work on the farm for a time.
9. Sam Oberholtzer
10. Zimmerman, Jane Metzler. *Elmer Nolt Metzler & Clara Martin Metzler: Their Commitment to Faith and Family (1897 - 1969).* Masthoff Press. 2016.
11. Based on conversations with the Oberholtzer bothers, many of whom worked on the farm in the late 1950s on up through the 1960s.
12. Based on conversations with Marlene Buch, the wife of Roy Buch Junior, a 7th generation decedent of Jacob N. Metzler.

Chapter 10: Harry Metzler Buch: Of Reformers, Shootings, and Shoes
1. Bowman, Sue. "Threshing Demonstration Provides a Look Back At Grain Harvesting's Labor-Intensive Past." *Intelligencer Journal/Lancaster New Era.* July 29, 2013. B5.
2. "Fire Destroyed Barn of Daniel Buch" *Lebanon Semi-Weekly News.* August 4, 1925.
3. Zimmerman, Jane Metzler. *Jacob Metzler and His Descendants.* 2013.
4. Field, Gene and Lucie Field. "Anthony Henkel." May 2011.

5. Stapleton, A. M.S., A.M., D.D. *The Henkel Memorial.* York, PA. 1910.
6. "Martin Luther." *Bio.* A&E Television Networks. 2016.
7. Zimmerman, Jane Metzler. *Elmer Nolt Metzler & Clara Martin Metzler: Their Commitment to Faith and Family (1897 - 1969).* Masthoff Press. 2016.
8. Zimmerman, Jane Metzler.
9. Zimmerman, Jane Metzler.
10. Zimmerman, Jane Metzler.
11. Zimmerman, Jane Metzler.
12. Sharp, John E. "Borough on a Hill: Akron, PA., 1915 - 1919." *Orie O. Miller Biography Project.* June 15, 2012.
13. Sharp.
14. Sharp.

Chapter 11: Kenneth Buch Hertzog: The End of a Farming Legacy

1. The farm had two cisterns when my father moved onto the farm in 1976. These would fill with rain water from the house. I remember them having water. Eventually my father filled them in and removed the concrete pads that topped them. When the summer becomes dry, the outline of these cisterns can still be seen.

Chapter 12: Kenneth Scott Hertzog: The Beginning of the Hertzog Homestead Bed and Breakfast

1. Horning, John B. "For Whom The School Bell Tools." *Lancaster Sunday News,* 2013.

Appendix I

My Connection to Martin Luther the Reformer

As I was compiling this book, local historian and educator David Sauder, who is also a descendant of Jacob Metzler, challenged me to provide a little bit more proof as to how I arrived at the conclusion that I was a descendant of Martin Luther, the great reformer. I knew I had independently verified it apart from the family trees one can sometimes find on Ancestry.com. The reality is that the family trees found on Ancestry.com are, at times, inaccurate. People place information online and do not verify it. And people want to feel like their lives are important and so sometimes they line up their family lines with knights or nobles from the medieval period. While I considered being related to Martin Luther a great honor, I wanted to do so with integrity and as much verification that I can. So here's a journey as to how I arrived at the conclusion that my family is descended from Martin Luther.

Martin Luther, born November 10, 1483 in Eisleben, Grafschaft Mansfeld, Heiliges Römisches Reich, married Katherina Von Bora, born January 29, 1499 in Lippendorf, Sachsen, Heiliges Römisches Reich, on June 27, 1525 in Wittenberg, Sachsen, Heiliges Römisches Reich. Their lives and parentages are fully documented in many histories, and I will not go into them here. According to Christian Historian Paul Thigpen, the Luther's had six children: Hans (June 7, 1526), Elizabeth (1527), Magdalena (1529), Martin (1531), Paul (1533), and Margaretha (1534).[1] Margaretha is the one we will follow.

Many online sources denote Margaretha as being married to Georg Von Kunheim, who was born in 1532. Still others claim that she was married to Johann Georg Claes Wagner who was born in 1520 and who died in 1553. Both seem to be right. Margaretha was married to Claes Wagner at the age of 15; Emmerich Wagner (1550) was born soon after. Claes Wagner would have been around 30 at the time, almost twice Margaretha's age.[2] He died three years later, and Margaretha meets Georg Von Kuenheim in Wittenberg who was sent to study law under the recommendation of Philipp Melanchthon. They married in 1555 and have 4 sons and 5 daughters of which 6 died in infancy. Margaretha and 5 of her children are buried before the altar of the church of Mühlhausen, Germany. She died on March, 3, 1570.[3]

Emmerich Wagner married Anna Von Steunburg (1545) who was 5 years his senior. According the Landeskirchliches Archive who used Ulrich Ehrbeck's book *Oberhessische Pfarrergeschichte ca. 1600 - 1966* and C. W. H. Hochhuth's book *Statistik der evangelischen Kirche im Regierungsbezirk Cassel*, Emmerich was a butcher by trade. They lived in Marberg.[4]

The archive goes onto state that Anna gave birth to a son they named Ludwig (1572). In 1587 Ludwig went onto study at the University of Marberg. He was involved in scholarly work from 1590 to 1604. In 1605, Ludwig was awarded a parish in Holzhausen, southeast of Marberg. He married Anna Holtshausen on July 17, 1608. She gave birth to a daughter Lousia Wagner on February 2, 1610.[5][6]

Apparently, around this time Count Moritz of Hesse-Kassel inherited the area. He desired to bring more reform to the church than Luther did. He wanted to reform the confession of Luther. Many Lutheran ministers, professors and teachers rejected the reformed confession. When it arrived at Holzhausen, Reverend Ludwig Wagner, abandoned his parish and for one year they had no leader.[7]

He traveled to Hesse-Darmstadt where Count Ludwig the V ruled. He happened to be a Lutheraner and a cousin of Count Moritz. In 1620, Ludwig Wagner was able to find a parish in the village of Stainbach, near Nähe der Stadt Gießen. So after this, Anna died and he remarried Elisabether Wentz on October 25, 1618. He experienced the first years of the 30 year war and dies in 1633.[8]

Lousia, also written as Loysa, Wagner, daughter of Ludwig Wagner, married Othmar Dentzer (August 17, 1595) on November 6, 1626. Othmar was an assistant Judge and a church Senior. He was the son of Simon Dentzer, the village mayor of Steinmerk, and

Eilalia Weiss.[9] Louisa gave birth to a daughter on June 6, 1640. She

was named Anna Eulalia Dentzer in honor of her grandmother.5

He also had 3 sons who also studied at Giessen University and

became Lutheran pastors.[10]

Eulalia Dentzer married Georg Henckel (1635) on May 2,

1666 in Steinberg, Oberhessen, Hessen, Germany. Georg enrolled

in the Fourth Class at Giessen University on July 25, 1650 from

Allendorf-ad-Lumbda. Georg was the village teacher and quite a

possibly a preacher. He became a schoolmaster in 1662. They

lived their lives in Mehreberg and had 6 children: Elisabetha,

Anthonius, Christianus, Konradus, Georg, and Philipp. Of these,

my line comes down through Anthonius Jacobus Henckel, who

was born in October 1668 and baptised on October 27, 1668.

Georg died 1678.[11]

Anthony Jacobus Henckel enrolled in Giessen University,

Giessen, Germany on May 5, 1688. Four years later on January 16,

1692, he faced examinations from the Theological Faculty of

Giessen and was soon after ordained. His ordination took place on

February 28, 1692 at Eschelbronn, Germany and it was here the he

took the position of parish pastor, a called laid on him by Baron

John Anton of Pfeltz. The following year, on February 23, 1693, he

was called to be the parish pastor of the church of Monchzell by

Baron John Melchoir of Vestenberg. A few years later on August

23, 1695, he was called by Baron Von Gemmingen to be the parish pastor of Daudenzell and Breitannbronn, Germany. He baptized 151 children, officiated 51 burials, and married 22 couples. In 1714, he was recalled by Baron John Melchoir of Vestenburg to the church at Monchzall. His final call in Germany came on October 11, 1714 when he was called to be the parish pastor of the Neckergemund and Zuzenhausen congregation. He served these churches until June 3, 1717 when he resigned and emigrated to Pennsylvania.[12]

Toward the end of Anthony Henckel's time in the old world, two things of note happened. During this time when a ruler of certain area in the Palatinate was Catholic, all the churches under him became Catholic; if he was protestant, that church was controlled by the churches. When Anthony was pastor at Daudenzell and Breitenbronn, protestants held the churches. When the electorate became Catholic, the electorate endeavored to have equal rights in all churches. In other words, the Catholics wanted to use the church half time. This happened to Anthony Henckel's parish in 1708 - 1709. He resisted this push, basing his resistance on an older ecclesiastical order, refusing to recognize the order come from the Catholic church. Eventually, a Catholic priest broke into the church with an axe. Anthony reported it to the patron of church who dropped the contest.[13]

A second incident occurred when Anthony Henkel appealed to Prince Ernst Ludwig, complained that Baron John Melchoir von Festenberg was using lands belonging to the church and keeping the tithes. The Baron denied everything and attacked the character on Henckel. It was this incident that potentially propelled him to America.[14]

It is believed that he arrived in America with his family on September 9, 1717 on board one of three ships: Captain Richmond landed with 164 passengers, Captain Toner (Tower) with 91 passengers, or Captain Eyers with 108 passengers.[15] According to "The Acta Historica Ecclesiatica", these vessels arrived filled with German Lutherans.[16]

Reverend Anthony Jacobus Henkel married Maria Elizabeth Dentzer in Germany, and they had 12 children. All were born in Germany. A complete listing of all of them can be found in *The Henckel Genealogy*. My line descends from his fourth child, Johann Gerhard Anthony Henkel, born on January 12, 1698 in Daudenzell, Germany. He was baptized on January 16 of the same year at the Evangelical Lutheran Church of Daudenzell.[17]

Gerhard was 19 when his parents emigrated to America. They settled on a New Hanover farm in Philadelphia (now Montgomery) County. He married Anna Catherine in 1720. He died in 1736 near Ephrata, Pennsylvania. She remarried on February 1, 1737 to a Thomas Wilson. She died in 1789.[18]

While records often confuse him with his father, we have no record of him ever being ordained. We do know that soon after his was married, on May 9, 1928, he purchased 192 acres of land from Maurice Morris of Abington, Philadelphia County. The location of this farm would be what is now considered Berks County which was formed in 1752. In the same year of the purchase he signed a petition to the authorities asking for protection from bands of marauding Indians.[19]

Around 1736, Gerhard and his son George Hinkle settle three miles south of Ephrata, in an area that became know as Hinkletown. His son George is the innkeeper at Hinkletown and built the first bridge over the Conestoga river there.[20]

Susanna Margaretha Henkel was the daughter of Gerhard Henkel, and was born about 1736 in Colebrookdale Township. She married Henry Miller Jr. on November 19, 1952. He was born May 12, 1728.[21]

She was the youngest child of Gerhard and Anna Catherina and was confirmed at the New Hanover Lutheran Church on April 8, 1750 at the age of 14 as the stepdaughter of Thomas Wilson.[22]

In 1710, the Cloisters of Ephrata, the first communistic enterprise in America, was formed. Hans Michael Muller an emigrant of 1710 from Strasburg along with his wife Barbara and 7 sons joined this organization. One of these sons, Heinrich Muller

Sr.(who was born in 1697 who died in 1757) and his wife Clara (who died in 1748), has a son named Henry Miller Jr., who was the husband of Susanna Henkel.[23] Heinrich Muller Sr. was baptized at the Cloister in 1728 and he was a householder there, appearing on tax lists in 1734, 1735, and 1738.[24]

Henry Miller Jr. was a brickmason and a builder and took a prominent part in the construction of the Ephrata Cloister buildings. During the period of dissatisfaction, he was able to trade his interest in the Cloister for 100 acres on nearby land. The house he built on this property eventually became the Smithton Inn, a bed and breakfast currently in operation today. His work as a brickmason extended down to and through the Revolutionary war. After the battle of Brandywine on September 11, 1777 about 50 miles from Ephrata, farmers from the area took wagons to the scene and returned with many of the sick and wounded. Documents should that "Medical staff, etc., (and) about 300 sick and wounded Continental Soldiers were brought here... The Sacred Saal of the Brotherhood (erected in 1740 as a place of worship)...soon became a charnel house. It witnessed scenes of woe and suffering seldom equaled. Within a few weeks...the deadly camp fever broke out and was soon beyond control." This resulted in the death of 60 soldiers and a large number of nurses and physicians.[25]

Henry Miller Jr. had two sons in the Patriot army and did not stand by. He helped minister to the needs of the sick and dying. He eventually took the deadly fever and died on January 12, 1778, buried in the Cloister Cemetery.[26]

One of these sons was Henry Miller III, who was born April 5, 1760 at the Ephrata Cloister, Ephrata, PA. He served in the Revolutionary War in the 5th Battalion, Lancaster County, Pennsylvania Militia. On April 1, 1783 he married Catherine Martin, daughter of John Martin. This was her second marriage; she had been married to Johannes Tischan (Deshong). She was born on November 24, 1758. When her sister-in-law died in 1806, she drove up to Jonestown in a sleigh and brought home all six of her children. She said that she had raised 14 children and guesses she could raise 6 more. She would actually go onto to raise only three of these children; others went to relatives. Henry Miller III died September 24, 1832 on the old homestead near Ephrata. His wife preceded him in death by four years, October 10, 1829.[27]

Henry Miller IV was born on January 11, 1784 in Lancaster County, PA. He married Catherine Miller, who was born on April 1, 1796 in North Carolina. He died August 21, 1866. She died March 5, 1868. Both were buried at Zion Hill, the Cloister Cemetery.[28]

They had one son, Peter Miller, who was born on January 2, 1814. He married Elizabeth Royer who was born April 2, 1816.

They had five children. My ancestor was John R. Miller, born on July 12, 1835.[29]

John R. Miller married Catherine Bollinger who was born on November 4, 1836. They had 6 children. One of these children was Catherine Bollinger Miller, who was known to most folks at Kate or Katie. She was born on September 9, 1870.[30]

She married Jacob Lane Hackman and they had 11 children. She was a housewife for 42 years. She eventually died of Uterine cancer, Carcinoma of the Uterus, something she suffered with for over two years.[31]

My great grandmother was born on December 29, 1889. Jacob and Katie named her Nora Miller Hackman. There are pictures of her holding me at the age of 2, though I do not remember her. She married Harry Metzler Buch. They had three children: Arlene, Eugene, and Roy. Arlene was my grandmother. She married Fred Hertzog. They had two children: Kenneth Buch Hertzog and Nancy Hertzog. Kenneth Hertzog married Arlene Hess. They had four children: Kenneth Scott, Douglas Kent, Jessica Kim, and Jason Daniel. Their stories are told elsewhere in this book.

1. Thigpen, Paul. "Martin Luther's Later Years: A Gallery - Family Album: Katherine Von Bora (1499–1552): Runaway nun who became Luther's "lord", *Christianity Today*. 1993. I used this source, but could have used many other sources.

2. Jacobsen, Alfred and Hanspeter, Werner. *The Descendants of the Reformer.* Page 330 and 364. July 29, 2015. Lutheriden Association. A Note: This work was key to determining a connection to Luther's daughter. Their resources are *Das Guldene und Silberne Ehren-Gedachnib Lutheri"* published in 1706; *Genealogia Lutherorum* published in 1733 by M. Davide Richter; David Keil's *Genealogie d.M. Luthers aus sicheren und zuverlassigen Nachrichten entworfen* publish 1731; the work of Prof. Dr. Karl Friedrich August Nobbe who lived from 1791 - 1878; the work of Pastor Otto Sartorius who lived from 1864 -1947; and Pastor Martin Clasen who lived from 1882 - 1962. The only information that might solidify this link with even more certainty would be documents indicating marriage, or baptismal certificates of Emmerich Wagner indicating parentage.

3. "History of Mühlhausen", *Ostpreussen.* 2011.

4. Ulrich Ehrbeck (Bearbeiter): *Oberhessische Pfarrergeschichte ca. 1600 - 1966.* Manuskript Wiesbaden 1995. Seite 186 f. and C. W. H. Hochhuth (Bearbeiter): *Statistik der evangelischen Kirche im Regierungsbezirk Cassel.* Kassel 1872. Seite 587 f. Georg Dehio: Handbuch der Deutschen Kunstdenkmäler: Hessen. 2. bearbeitete Au age. München 1982. Seite 730 und 834.

5. Ulrich.

6. Jacobsen, Alfred and Hanspeter, Werner.

7. Ulrich.

8. Ulrich.

9. Junkin, William Junkin and Minnie Wyatt Junkin. The Henckel Genealogy, 1500 -1960. Ancestry and Descendants of Reverend Anthony Jacob Henckel 1668 - 1728. 1964.

10. Junkin.

11. Junkin.

12. Junkin.

13. Junkin.

14. Junkin.

15. Diffenderfer, Frank Reid. German Immigration to Pennsylvania, 1900. Page 39.

16. Wiemer. The Acta Historica Ecclesiastica. Volume 41, Page 1054, 1738.

17. Junkin.

18. Junkin.

19. Junkin.

20. Junkin.

21. Junkin.

22. Junkin.

23. Junkin.

24. Brother Kenan's Notebook (Deaths and Other Occurrences), page 58, 1748.

25. Junkin.

26. Junkin.

27. Junkin.

28. Junkin.

29. Junkin.

30. Kate B. Hackman's Death Certificate.

31. Kate B. Hackman's Death Certificate.

Referenced: Henkel, Elon. Henckel Family Records. 1635-1939, p 129, 130.